OVERFLOW

OVERFLOW

How the Joy of the Trinity
Inspires Our Mission

Michael Reeves

MOODY PUBLISHERS
CHICAGO

Edited by Pamela Joy Pugh
Interior design: Brandi Davis
Cover design: Derek Thornton / Notch Design
Cover image of waves copyright © 2014 by Benjamin Schedler / Stocksy (331016). All rights reserved.

Library of Congress Cataloging-in-Publication Data

Names: Reeves, Michael (Michael Richard Ewert), author.
Title: Overflow : how the joy of the Trinity inspires our mission / Michael Reeves.
Description: Chicago : Moody Publishers, 2021. | Includes bibliographical references. | Summary: "The Trinity has everything to do with the practice of missions. When we see the love of the Father, Son, and Holy Spirit that overflows into creation, missions won't be a chore. Instead, delighted by the abundance of God's love, we who have received it delight to tell the world"-- Provided by publisher.
Identifiers: LCCN 2021003061 (print) | LCCN 2021003062 (ebook) | ISBN 9780802422613 | ISBN 9780802499417 (ebook)
Subjects: LCSH: Trinity. | Missions. | Joy--Religious aspects--Christianity.
Classification: LCC BT111.3 .R447 2021 (print) | LCC BT111.3 (ebook) | DDC 266--dc23
LC record available at https://lccn.loc.gov/2021003061
LC ebook record available at https://lccn.loc.gov/2021003062

Originally delivered by fleets of horse-drawn wagons, the affordable paperbacks from D. L. Moody's publishing house resourced the church and served everyday people. Now, after more than 125 years of publishing and ministry, Moody Publishers' mission remains the same—even if our delivery systems have changed a bit. For more information on other books (and resources) created from a biblical perspective, go to www.moodypublishers.com or write to:

Moody Publishers
820 N. LaSalle Boulevard
Chicago, IL 60610

1 3 5 7 9 10 8 6 4 2

Printed in the United States of America

To

Martha
Jemma
Nicole
Danielle
Daisy
Eliza
Sylvia
Timothy

This is the joy I want for you.

CONTENTS

INTRODUCTION
Knowing the Triune God
9

CHAPTER 1
God's Love: The Fountain of All Goodness
15

CHAPTER 2
God's Glory: The Radiance of the World
39

CHAPTER 3
God's Abundance: The Barren Land of No Trinity
59

CHAPTER 4
God's Light: Shining in the Darkness
79

NOTES
97

KNOWING THE TRIUNE GOD

That is the bizarre thing about the good news: who knows how you will really hear it one day, but once you have heard it, I mean really heard *it, you can never* unhear *it.*

CAROLYN WEBER

P erhaps I should have called this book *From Drudgery to Delight*, because that's my aim here. I want you to step out from any begrudging, bored, going-through-the-motions religion into a heartfelt happiness in Christ.

I've been through that change, and I know where it comes from. It comes from knowing God as Trinity. Now, I'd known that God was Father, Son, and Spirit for years, but it had seemed to me like a bit of mere stained-glass decoration on Christianity. In other words, the Trinity was there, it was even mildly interesting as an idea, but it didn't *do* anything. It was just pretty window dressing.

But when I came to appreciate who God is and saw that God's being Father, Son, and Spirit is why He *is* glorious Love, I saw how different the triune God is from all my bored and fearful ideas of God: that's when I started to *adore* Him. He became staggeringly delightful and precious to me. That's when He became more lovely to me even than the thought of going to someplace called heaven. He—and not some abstract reward of "eternal life"—became the center of my hope and joy. And that's when I started, instinctively, to rave about God. Knowing God as Trinity started me speaking with relish of God. The Trinity pushed me beyond a tick-the-box-of-duty evangelism into a fuller life of intentional mission with glee. And that's what I want for you with this book. I want you to know a God who is not mean and pinched but overflowing with life, goodness, and beauty. For when you are full of Him, you too will overflow and be a spring of life-giving water to all around you.

So this book is for those who feel spiritually empty and discouraged. It's for those who feel the sneaking suspicion that God must be fed up with them. For those who hardly dare think it, but sense that God is a bit of a bore, a demanding boss who just wants to take from us. For those who feel unworthy or unable ever to tell others of Jesus. For those who just don't find God interesting enough to want to shout about Him to the world. My aim is to take you to the fountain of life so that you can be refreshed and so satisfied in Him that you cannot keep it in: you overflow to the world.

The substance of this book comes from three addresses given at the Moody Bible Institute's Missions Conference in the fall of 2019. It seemed appropriate material for that event, given how the extraordinary evangelistic and mission work of D. L. Moody all started in a Boston shoe store on April 21, 1855, when Edward Kimball told him of Christ's love for him. And who was Edward Kimball? A workingman who taught the Sunday school class seventeen-year-old Dwight Moody attended, who overflowed with a loving God and went on mission to visit his student at the shoe store where he worked.

It was the knowledge of such a loving God and Savior that turned Moody inside out, transforming a self-obsessed man into a blazing star of the gospel. You may be the Edward Kimball in someone's life. Or you may be called to a different arena, as Moody was. But in the pages of this book, we will get to know the living God as Trinity and why that matters. We'll see why He is so beautiful that we can't help overflowing with love for Him and bringing His love to others. That's our privilege and our mission.

The great nineteenth-century London preacher Charles Spurgeon once said this:[1]

> The most excellent study for expanding the soul, is the science of Christ, and him crucified, and the knowledge of the Godhead in the glorious Trinity. Nothing will so enlarge the intellect, nothing so magnify the whole soul of man, as a devout, earnest, continued investigation of the great subject of the Deity. And, whilst humbling and expanding, this subject is eminently *consolatory*. Oh, there is, in contemplating Christ, a balm for every wound; in musing on the Father, there is a quietus for

every grief; and in the influence of the Holy Ghost, there is a balsam for every sore. Would you lose your sorrows? Would you drown your cares? Then go, plunge yourself in the Godhead's deepest sea; be lost in his immensity; and you shall come forth as from a couch of rest, refreshed and invigorated. I know nothing which can so comfort the soul; so calm the swelling billows of grief and sorrow; so speak peace to the winds of trial, as a devout musing upon the subject of the Godhead.

That is what I want us to do now. In the first chapter, we will get to know the living God: Father, Son, and Spirit. We are going to see that the Trinity is not a weird puzzle for theological nerds but glorious good news for every Christian to enjoy. We will see that, *precisely because God is triune*, His very being is found in giving, not taking. He is a God of overflowing super-abundance, which is why (unlike the gods of human religion and our imagination) He always acts with such utter graciousness.

In the second chapter I want to delve a little deeper by looking at the Bible's grand drama as the story of God's outgoing glory, from the darkness of Genesis 1 to the light of Revelation 22. Through it we will see the radiantly self-giving nature of God as the wellspring of all love, joy, goodness—and mission.

From there, in the third chapter, we will change tack to think about what reality is like when the Trinity is denied. That might sound like it will make for a very short chapter, but actually, what people make of ultimate reality shapes every part of their lives. Belief in a different sort of god—or no God at all—

will have the profoundest of consequences. We will see that when the Trinity is denied, love is denied, and people are forced either into the worship of loveless and frightening idols, or into a despairing nihilism and meaninglessness.

Then, in the last chapter, the book will conclude with a look at how, when Christians share God's own outgoing fullness and radiance, we shine as lights in this current darkness. And note well the "we" there. For it is not just the extraordinarily gifted "A-list" Christians—the D. L. Moodys and the Martin Luthers—who can shine like stars, bright and beaming. It is ordinary failures full of mess, like you and me.

So, my friend, come with me now to the loving Friend of sinners, the glorious God of love, and see if some time spent contemplating Him can brighten and lift you and make you overflow. Let's go!

On Reflection

1. The book opens with "I want you to step out from any begrudging, bored, going-through-the-motions religion into a heartfelt happiness in Christ." When have you experienced a "heartfelt happiness in Christ"?

2. "He—and not some abstract reward of 'eternal life'—became the center of my hope and joy." Have you had a similar experience to what the author describes here?

3. Having read the description of the upcoming four chapters, what intrigues you about embracing a fuller understanding of the triune God?

CHAPTER 1

GOD'S LOVE
The Fountain of All Goodness

Scripture repeatedly proclaims that God is love. Our hearts long for His love to be boldly reflected in our lives. A love that is true, good, faithful, joyful, unsullied, unchanging, and unceasing. This love is evidenced solely in and through God the Father, Son, and Holy Spirit.

KATHERINE ELIZABETH CLARK

This is a book about the Holy Trinity and Christian missions. Now, when you read those words on the page, or when you first saw them on the cover, it might have prompted the question "What kind of crazy man writes a book about that? The Trinity and missions? What do they have to do with each other?" It's a bit like writing a book about sushi and spaceships, or rugby and rattlesnakes, or crocheting and chaos theory. Those things just don't go together, no matter how hard you try to pair them. Or so you might think.

But then perhaps you are reminded that the Trinity and missions aren't totally unrelated. A key Christian doctrine like the Trinity and an obvious Christian obligation like evangelism—they're in the same ballpark, right? They both come under the same "big tent" at the religious circus. Somehow they are related. But how?

Perhaps the Trinity is for one kind of Christian, while missions is for another. Those tweed-jacketed fellows called "theologians" must think long and hard about the Trinity while stroking their beards as they sit beside the fireplace. Meanwhile, the hard-charging, pith-helmeted missionaries with machetes in one hand and a Bible in the other are clearing the jungle and making a way for the gospel. Both tasks are God things, in their own way. They're *sort of* related to each other, right? Yes, perhaps they are—though not by much, we suspect.

This sort of thinking comes because we don't view the Trinity as practical, or at least not as practical as good old-fashioned soul-saving on the front lines. I think most Christians feel that there is the God whom we know and love and sort of understand—and then there is the Trinity. And the Trinity is, well, it only matters somewhere over there in the ivy-covered seminaries. It's really just for those pasty-faced, socially disastrous theologians. They're the ones who like to talk about Trinity. And when that has befuddled them enough, they switch to talking about how many angels can dance on the head of a pin. (That's a real thing, actually. Medieval theologians debated the issue. Maybe some theologians still do.) So that's how the Trinity must be as well. Fusty graybeards debating how $1 + 1 + 1 = 1$, and all that. *But come on, that's just not relevant to anyone now,* we think.

Deep in the Christian psyche today is this idea—a dangerous and mistaken idea—that the Trinity is a wart on our knowledge of God. It's an irrelevance. And you can see it when you see Christians actually sharing their faith. Just think about a Christian sharing the gospel for the first time. What is it you expect to hear? You expect to hear about the cross, about God's grace, about forgiveness. It's all about Jesus, because who doesn't like Jesus, right? I mean, He would pet soft lambs, and He looked so cute lying in that manger. And He came to give you God's gift of salvation so you can go to heaven. Those are the sort of things you expect to hear from first-time witnesses. But I don't expect them to be clear about *which* God they are talking about to the unbeliever. And I certainly don't expect them to be clear on the Trinity—or even to bring up the concept. Why would you confuse the simple gospel message with a bunch of extraneous metaphysics?

And so, across the West today, we rhapsodize over the beauty of the gospel but perhaps neglect the beauty of the God whose gospel it is. So what we are going to contemplate now, as the first order of business, is that God is lovely precisely because God is triune.

THE GOD WHO IS MISSION

My goal in this book is for the Christian to enjoy the extraordinary and beautiful truth that mission—which is about going *out*, whether nearby or to a foreign land—is not something alien to who God is. It is not that mission is, "Well, unfortunately, we have to go out and do all the hard work of evangelizing while God enjoys Himself up there in heaven, leaning back on His throne listening to angel songs." That ain't it. No. Never was, and never will be.

Mission is rooted in the Trinity, in the very being and nature and heart of God. And this is something deeply heart-winning and attractive in Him. If there is one thing I really want, above all, to communicate in this book, it is the great truth that God is mission. Wherever you're at with God, particularly if you aren't too thrilled with Him at the moment, I'd love for your eyes to be opened so you see just how stunningly beautiful and satisfying He is. I pray that your heart begins—maybe for the first time in a long time, maybe for the first time ever—to burn with a love for Him. Not just a duty that compels you and tells you what you ought to do, but rather, that you truly *love* Him! And then, out of this deep love, you will want to see the whole world come to know about Him too.

> I WANT FIRST AND FOREMOST FOR YOU TO LOVE GOD, SO THAT YOUR MISSION IS NOTHING OTHER THAN SPEAKING TO THE WORLD ABOUT WHO YOU LOVE.

Some of you reading this have gone away from your home and the familiar for the purpose of missions—reaching people in another culture or another land with the Christian faith. Or perhaps you are training for a cross-cultural mission. Others of you are living missionally where you are. Your purpose is to be intentional in reaching your neighborhood, family, workplace with whatever evangelistic opportunities open themselves to you. But either way, I do not want you, dear friend, to just go out on mission. That gets talked about a lot today. It's a way of making Christianity seem exciting, like an adventure that you undertake with faithful comrades. It's like heading out to the mountains with a backpack of provisions and Aragorn at your side. You're joining some friends to go save the world. Who wouldn't want to be part of a mission like that?

But going out on mission is not the primary thing; it is a secondary thing. I want first and foremost for you to love God so that your mission is nothing other than speaking to the world about who you love. To go on God's mission is to speak of Him out of a heart that is captivated by His beauty. And to do this, we must know who He is. So I want to start by thinking simply, by asking, "Who exactly is this God who shapes mission?" And our answer is that He is the triune God, for only a triune God can be truly missional—not just as a mission sender, but missional in His own being.

GETTING TO KNOW THE TRINITY

Where do we start when we want to think about the Trinity? Typically, since this doctrine is not well understood by us, and because it describes the infinite God, we immediately try to illustrate it with things from our world. We try to explain the supernatural by reference to the natural. Unfortunately, this is where so many go wrong. Because as soon as people hear the word "Trinity," all these weird illustrations immediately spring to mind.

You know how it is. In a Bible study group in your church, an unsuspecting new Christian says, "Please, can somebody explain the Trinity to me?"

And then someone goes, "Ah, yes. Well, you see, the infinite God is like a three-leaf clover. There is one leaf, yet three leaflets make it up. Three making one. I find this example so helpful."

And someone else says, "No, no, no. God is like H_2O. There is ice, but then you warm up the Father and He gets a bit more liquid—a different state of matter, a different mode of being—and you warm Him up a bit more, and He is spiritual, you know."

Or my favorite: "God is like an egg. There is the yolk. There is the white. And the shell. Three parts. Yet at the same time . . . wait for it . . . it's just one egg." Ta-da!

Is *anyone* going to bow down on their faces because of the "eggishness" of God?

And that's why you think, "Of course not. That's why I want to leave all the weirdness to the theologians."

Friend, we Christians believe in the Trinity not because we sense God's similarity with things from our backyard, or our stove top, or our breakfast table, but because of the Lord Jesus Christ.

Know Jesus, Know the Trinity

John 20:31 is John's mission statement, the purpose of writing his gospel. He is telling us why he has written what he has. That verse says, "these [words] are written so that you may believe that Jesus is the Christ, the Son of God, and that by believing you may have life in his name." John asks you to put your faith in Jesus. It's just a simple call to faith. But do you see what he has done? A simple call to faith in Jesus is a call to faith in a triune God. How so? Because Jesus is the Christ, the Messiah. What does that word mean? The Anointed One, that is, He who is anointed with the Spirit. Acts 10:38 says, "God anointed Jesus of Nazareth with the Holy Spirit and with power." The reality of the Holy Spirit is implicit in John's term, "the Christ." Then look what else John says: Jesus is the "Son of God." In other words, God is His Father. All three persons of the Trinity are here! This sort of thing is everywhere in the Bible, once you have the eyes to see it.

The fact is, looking at the Trinity is simply pressing in to know who Jesus is.

God the Loving Father

A good way to begin to understand the triune God is to ponder these statements: Before God created the world, was He idle? Was He active? If He wasn't idle, just what was He doing? Have you ever asked these sorts of questions? You know there's got to be a pompous theological answer, right? So what *was* God doing before He created the world? If anyone ever asks, here's a possible response: "You know, actually, John 17:24 tells us what God was doing back then. Jesus says, 'Father . . . you loved me before the foundation of the world.'" That is the God we are talking about. A God who is a Father, who has been eternally loving His Son.

Now, what does it mean that God is a Father? In Scripture, names are always meaningful. My name is Mike. But it could be Billy. It really doesn't matter. It doesn't tell you anything about me. Put any name on the cover of this book and it wouldn't make any difference. But when God is called Father, it is important because He *actually is* a Father. It's not just a convention by which we designate Him. It's a descriptor of His being. He is God the Father. And a father is someone who, giving life, lavishes love on his children. And if before all things God was eternally a Father, well, then, quite inevitably: God is eternally a life-giving, loving God.

May I pause here for a moment? You might be someone whose earthly father was cold or distant or aloof. Perhaps your father hurt you or caused you great pain. And so every time I write that word and you see it on the page, it makes you shrink into a shell because of what you have experienced. The word *father* is not good news to you. Dear friend, if that is you, God the Father is not called Father because He is like your dad. Earthly fathers are meant to be like this Father, but we all fail. Some catastrophically. So don't describe God the Father from what your dad was like and how he failed. Friend, the reason it hurts so much for you is because *father* should be such a sweet word for you, and you have been hurt, and that grieves me. And I grieve especially for you, right now, as you are being asked to look at the fatherhood of God. I want this book to be a balm for you. I want its message to help you. So try to look at the term afresh and find its meaning reconstructed for you. Find the loveliness in the heavenly Father that perhaps you never enjoyed in your earthly father.

Let us consider some well-known words about the Father in 1 John 4. We will focus attention on verses 7–8: "Beloved, let us love one another, for love is from God, and whoever loves has been born

GOD IS LOVE IN SUCH A PROFOUND AND IMPORTANT WAY; YOU JUST CANNOT KNOW HIM WITHOUT BECOMING LOVING.

of God and knows God. Anyone who does not love does not know God, because God is love." Notice what this passage says: Whoever loves knows God, because God is love.

Have you ever known a dear saint who has been walking with the Lord for years, who just seems to ooze joyfulness and love and generosity and compassion and kindness? And you think, *I want to be like that when I am seventy.* Someone whose very presence is gold. You go out for Sunday lunch with them after church or are invited to lunch at their place, and when you are with them, you start finding that you're really nice around them. Right? Because they are never mean about people behind their backs. And just while you're with them, you start actually being nicer. (You revert later, of course!) But while you're with them, they change you.

This is a simple picture of how God is, according to John. God is love, and He is love in such a deep and powerful way that when you know Him you also will become loving. You couldn't not be loving. You become what He is. This is what it means that God is Father. John's words in verse 8, "God is love," refer to God the Father. Do you see the next words? Verse 9: "In this the love of God was made manifest among us, that God sent his only Son into the world, so that we might live through him." So the God who is love is the Father who sends His Son. *To be Father means to love.* To give out life, to beget the Son. Without love, He would not be who He is. He would not be Father. He would not have a Son to rain a cascade of love over. Simply put, this God is love. To be Father means to have a Son and to love Him eternally.

Images of God's Bountiful Love

As you might know, there are a couple of images that theologians like to use for describing the bounty of God's love. One is a scriptural image of the Lord as a fountain of life. And as theologians enjoy pointing out, for God to be a fountain, His living water must bubble over. That's what fountains do. They don't merely trickle parsimoniously. They generously shoot out their contents! So for the Father to be who He is, He must pour out life and love.

Another image is the shining sun. By nature of being the sun, it must give out life. Its very rays are life-giving. If you were to put down a tarp in your yard, the grass under it would wither and die. Grass can't grow in the dark. But if you shine light on grass, it grows. Just so with this God of ours, He must ever blaze out with love. And as with grass, water is needed too. Both of these things pour out health and life for living things. That is our God! So now, my friend, you begin to see why the Trinity is such good news.

And why is God love? He is love because He is Trinity. And you get an image of this in the baptism of Jesus. If you want an illustration of the Trinity to share, use this one rather than the one about eggs.

Perhaps you remember this story in Luke 3, the baptism of Jesus. Jesus is there in the waters of the Jordan River, and He hears those words: "You are my beloved Son; with you I am well pleased." And what have I left out? Is there only a heavenly voice? Is the scene otherwise empty? No, the Holy Spirit is also there, resting on Jesus in bodily form like a dove. That's the God we are talking about. The Father who pours out the Spirit of His love, making His love known to the Son. And the Son, how does He feel about it? There is this lovely moment in Luke 10:21 where Jesus is said to be full of joy in the Holy Spirit, and He cries, "I praise you, Father, Lord of heaven and earth" (NIV). Because the Father has poured out so much love on Jesus, all He can do is echo this love back to His Father. That is the God we are talking about.

My friend, I hope you have begun to see that when you start with Jesus, the triune God that He makes known is not a weird math problem in which three must equal one, or a philosophical brain twister that makes your head spin. A Father who gives life with love to His Son in fellowship with the Spirit. That's the real God. When you start with Jesus, and in Him you discover a triune God, you have found a God of infinite beauty, love, and loveliness beyond compare.

WHAT IF GOD WERE NOT TRINITY?

Only a triune God can have this kind of incomparable beauty. To understand this a little bit more, I invite you to do a short mental exercise. Right now, wherever you are sitting, just close your eyes for a moment. Imagine you're God. Now why would you, in your divine wisdom and power, create a universe? What would be your reason? Why would you do it? Is it because you are lonely and you'd fancy having some friends? Or is it that you think, "Hey, I can have some slaves. I can have some servants to do whatever I want"? Is it because you want to be pampered? (You can open your eyes now.) How did you do? Did you come up with any noble reasons?

It is one of the profoundest questions that philosophers ask: Is there a God? And if so, following that, why is there anything else? Why the universe? Why us? Why would God decide to have a creation? This actually isn't just a philosophical debate. All thoughtful humans have struggled to answer these enduring questions.

The Nature of a Single-Person God

One of the earliest attempts to deal with these matters was given in a favorite illustration of mine, the Babylonian creation myth, the Enuma Elish. Here the god Marduk says he will create humanity because he wants to have slaves who will simply serve him. From then on, in early human religions, many gods have tended to like Marduk's approach: "I will create people to have servants." Now that is quite an attractive vision if you are a god.

It puts him in charge like a god feels he should be. And it turns worship into what we humans would want to receive ourselves: slavish devotion to a dominant master.

Why is it that the gods of most human religions are believed to think like this? Well, imagine a god who is the origin and cause of everything. He brought everything into existence. What was he like before he created the world? Just picture him in your mind. This god is sitting on his throne, but he hasn't yet created anything. So I guess he's not actually sitting on a throne, is he? He's just there, squatting in empty space. What is this god's character? You could say, "I don't know. How could I possibly know what he is like?" But there is one thing you do know. He is all alone, completely and totally alone, without even a throne. He is utterly lonely. Solitary. For all eternity past.

FOR A GOD WHO IS JUST INTERESTED IN HIMSELF, WOULDN'T A UNIVERSE BE AN IRRITATING DISTRACTION? HE JUST WANTS TO THINK ABOUT HIMSELF THE WHOLE TIME.

And so for eons and eons, this solitary god has had nobody and nothing to love. This means that love for others cannot be the essential characteristic of a single-person god. Love cannot be his defining attribute, because there is no other for such a god to love. He might love himself. But we don't call that love—we call it selfishness. At its worst, we call it psychotic narcissism.

And so by his very nature, a single-person god must be fundamentally inward looking, and therefore not loving. This being is essentially about private self-gratification. And that is the only reason why he creates. That is the sort of problem in every human religion with non-triune gods. Because single-person gods have spent eternity by themselves, they are almost unavoidably self-centered. How could they be anything else? And why would they desire to generate any other being— wouldn't that just be an annoying diversion? A single-person god prefers to think about himself. Creating looks odd in such religious worldviews. And if single-person gods do create, it is always out of a neediness. A desire for something beyond himself, a loneliness within his being. A desire to have friends or a desire to have servants. And it is only different with a triune God. When we're talking about the Father, Son, and Holy Spirit, everything changes. Now we have a God who certainly is not lonely but who, forever, has been in the business of loving. He is the Father who has loved the Son through the fellowship of the Spirit. Think of God the Father, whose very nature is to be loving and life-giving.

Why Our God Creates

One of my favorite old Puritan preachers is Richard Sibbes. He used to be called the "honey-mouthed" and the "sweet-dropper" for the sheer kindheartedness of his sermons. He once put it like this: "If God had not a communicative, spreading goodness, he would never have created the world. The Father, Son, and Holy Ghost were happy in themselves, and enjoyed one another before the world was. Apart from the fact that God delights to communicate and spread his goodness, there had never been a creation or redemption."[1] Sibbes was saying that

God didn't *need* to create the world in order to satisfy Himself or to be happy. The Father, Son, and Spirit "were happy in themselves, and enjoyed one another before the world was."

So why did God create? Because God delights to spread His goodness. In other words, He is like a sun of goodness, blazing out with love. God didn't create because He needed to, because of any lack. He created because He was so happily bursting with goodness. God is so overflowingly, super-abundantly full of life in Himself that He delighted to spread His goodness. His innermost being is a sun of light, life and warmth, always shining *out*: radiant and outgoing.

Now, if you have a god who is not a father, would such a barren god be capable of creating? You have no such doubts with a Father who has eternally been life-giving, because with such a God, it is unsurprising that He should create. So Jesus Christ is the logic of creation. If you want to get the nature of God, remember that Jesus Christ the Son is the one eternally loved of the Father, and creation is an outward expansion of that love. His love is like a fountain, spilling out, not kept for Himself, but splashing over others. So delighted with His Son was the Father that His love overflowed. This beloved Son was to be the firstborn of countless offspring. That was God's aim. As Paul put it in Romans 8:29, "For those whom [God] foreknew he also predestined to be conformed to the image of his Son, in order that he might be the firstborn among many brothers." This is a God who need not resent another beside Him. No, he exults in it! It is His joy to flood His Son with love and, through creating, He exults in flooding His many offspring with His love.

There is something that Jesus says at the end of His High Priestly Prayer, which captures what it means to be the Son. Right at the end of John 17, Jesus explains why He has come. In the very last verse of the chapter, verse 26, He is praying earnestly, and He says to His Father, "I made known to them your name, and I will continue to make it known, that *the love with which you have loved me may be in them,* and I in them." And Jesus also said in John 17:23 that God loves His followers just as He loves His only Son. No other god can offer that, such a glorious welcome, a Father welcoming us as His children. We are brought into the divine love with total acceptance. No other religion offers that kind of welcome. All this is to say, dear friend, that the nature of the triune God is totally different than the nature of all other gods.

THAT IS THE REASON WHY GOD IS SO LOVELY, THE REASON WHY WE WOULD WANT TO GO OUT AND SPEAK ABOUT HIM.

This is summarized really well in C. S. Lewis's *The Screwtape Letters.* If that isn't a book you've read, you should. Lewis contrasts the devil, who is the definitive single-person god, with the God who pours forth His fountain of love. In this book, Screwtape, who is an imaginary demon of some rank within Satan's forces, writes to a lesser demon to give advice about their enemy, God. And Screwtape gets it right when he says,

One must face the fact that all the talk about His love for men, and His service being perfect freedom, is not (as one would gladly believe) mere propaganda, but an appalling truth. He really *does* want to fill the universe with a lot of loathsome little replicas of Himself—creatures, whose life, on its miniature scale, will be qualitatively like His own, not because He has absorbed them but because their wills freely conform to His. We want cattle who can finally become food; He wants servants who can finally become sons. We want to suck in, He wants to give out. We are empty and would be filled; He is full and flows over.[2]

Screwtape is appalled by the God he sees, but he is exactly right!

And friend, the tragedy is that so many people think that the living God is the devilish one. Particularly when it comes to mission. As if God simply wants to get, to take. As if He goes on mission like it's a conquest instead of an overture of love. But the dissimilarity between the devil and the triune God simply could not be more stark. Where the devil is envious, grasping, always taking—and by the way, this is why sin will never satisfy, because it will not produce the satisfaction it promises but is always taking from you, promising only to steal—the living God, in contrast to the devil, is super-abundant, life-giving in His very nature. God is generous. He is outgoing. In fact, love is not a reaction with this God, for He takes the initiative.

And that is the origin of all mission. That is the reason why God is so lovely, the reason why we would want to go out and speak about Him. And it is the reason why we do. Remember, the essential nature of God is love—not stingy love, but generous love like a fountain splashing out joyfully. This bountiful God's gladness is enriched by having His Son at His side. He created that His love would be teeming, that it might be shared with His created image bearers, so that His Son might be the firstborn among many. Creation is the beginning of a spreading, an outward explosion of love. This God is the very opposite of Satan's greedy, hungry, selfish emptiness.

MISSION FLOWS FROM ABUNDANT LOVE

If you think that Christian life or mission is fundamentally some duty you've got to begrudgingly undertake, my dear friend, you've not got it. You've not understood who this God is. And if you want to see the difference between grudging, reluctant mission that is simply doing what you think you ought to do, and hilariously cheerful, delightful, life-laying-down mission, the secret is found in knowing who our God is. You must see that this God is not demanding stuff from you simply for His own pleasure but that your mission started in who He is.

God is so overflowingly gracious and loving that He started the love by loving you! When you were lost and far away, "while we were still sinners," as Paul says, Christ Jesus died for us (Rom. 5:8). Our mission is joining in God's life. We first discover how gracious He has been and we see how loving He is. Then we get to share His joy as we go out. Everything about this God is gracious and overflowing. It is why He created and why He saves. Because He is a God who *delights* to show mercy.

Psalm 19:1 reminds us, "The heavens declare the glory

of God." And it is easy to read that and think, "Why did God create? Well, the Bible says the heavens declare the glory of God, so I guess I am seeing God's immensity, His divine power over nature." Next time you get a chance, look up at the night sky and contemplate that you are not *only* seeing the might of the Creator in those stars. Power is not the only thing we see in the vastness of the universe. God's power tells us how He created; it does not tell us why.

Think of a time when you gazed at the sky on a very dark night. So many stars! God didn't merely sprinkle a few stars about. No, His way is to explode the heavenly skies with billions! And not just to awe you with the greatness of His handiwork but as an expression of His kind generosity. He also put clouds in the sky that drop down rain. He placed a sun in the sky that gives warmth and life and light to the world. He created a moon as a light in the darkness so that night would not be blindness for us. He created every molecule of air, minuscule packets of nitrogen and oxygen that you breathe every second so you do not suffocate.

That is why God created, out of a sheer overflow of magnanimity, to give you what you need, and more than what you need, for life and health and enjoyment of this world.

When next you gaze up at the sky and notice clouds, the moon, the stars, bear in mind that this great canopy is there as a result of God being a God of magnanimous love. That these great bodies remain where they are shows us that His love is unceasing. And not only is His love lavished upon monumental creations but it is also attentive to you and to me. This is a God who knows the number of hairs on your head, who heeds the fall of even the common sparrow. And through His love, all this is sustained through His Son, breathed through His Spirit. That is the origin of creation: the love and generosity of God. It is the reason for salvation too, the reason for mission. All love flows out of who God is. The compassion we show for the lost and the weak and the dying is an overflow, an expression of that first love, which is sourced in God. In the Trinity, we see the love behind all love, the joy behind all joy, the life behind all life. This is the origin of all going out and of all compassion.

This is how Martin Luther put it: "The love of God does not find, but creates, that which is pleasing to it. . . . Rather than seeking its own good, the love of God flows forth and bestows good. Therefore"—this was written over five hundred years ago, but it could have been written for us right now—"sinners are attractive because they are loved; they are not loved because they are attractive."[3]

This may not seem like an easy concept, but really, it is. Think how the media deluge us with the message that by becoming more attractive—buy this product, emulate that celebrity—you will be loved more. But not so with God. Let Martin Luther's words rest in you: "Sinners are attractive because they are loved," not the inverse. And you must know, dear friend, that this God knows the very depths of your heart, knows your dirtiness and the things that shame you. In fact, He knows far more about you than you do. You may feel that there is a dirtiness and a shame that people around you don't know, and it would make you beyond grace. No. Not so. Not with a triune God because this God is so loving in His nature, He is a God who *delights to show mercy.*

Know this, dear friend: there is more power in Christ's blood than there is in all of your sin. Do these words strike your heart as you read them? Right now, if there is any coldness in you, any sin unconfessed, rather than try to cover it up and hide it from Christ, why not hold it out to Him? Let Him prove Himself to you right now as a glorious Redeemer, and experience for yourself that this God is a gracious Savior to broken, messed-up failures like you and me. And when you see that's how loving and good our God is, then you think, "If He really loves me, not the outer mask, but me . . . if there is more power in His grace than there is in my sin . . . what a God!" Here is a

> **ONLY WITH THE TRINITY DO WE HAVE A GOD CAPABLE OF OFFERING TRULY GOOD NEWS.**

God more delightful and satisfying than anything else the world offers. Here is a God worth celebrating before all the world.

Only with the Trinity do we have a God capable of offering truly good news. Only with the Trinity can we have a desire to go out in mission, not grudging, but rejoicing, knowing He's the one who is merciful, He's the one who is beautiful. God has shown mercy and beauty and grace even to someone such as me. And because He is so good and better than anything else, I desire to share Him with all the world, however I might be called upon to do so.

How do you gain this wonder and awe? You must push in to know God better, get on your knees and pray that you might know Him more. Open the Scriptures and ask that you might see wonderful things in those pages. Ask to behold God's beauty so that you might quake in wonder at His love. And then you will find shame replaced by love, guilt replaced by joy, and you will be swept along, wanting to see the glory of God's love and kindness dispel the darkness of our world.

The triune God is where mission starts. If you will press in to know Him, you will be swept out of guilt and drudgery and into a delighted sharing of His mission. That is what I long for you to discover in the pages of this book. I want to see you get rid of your reluctant guilt and know this beautiful God. Have Him as your Savior and Redeemer. Know that He truly loves people who have failed and is sufficient to forgive their every sin. Then, forgiven and freed, you will want to go out and sing His praises to the world.

On Reflection

1. What is your understanding of *mission*? Why does the author say going out on mission is secondary, not primary? Explain his reasoning. What *is* primary?

2. Some Christian traditions just don't discuss the Trinity much. What has been your understanding of the Trinity? How do you respond to some of the illustrations that attempt to explain how the Trinity "works"?

3. Why is it so significant that God is called Father? Describe your results with the mental exercise: "Imagine you're God. Now why would you, in your divine wisdom and power, create a universe? What would be your reason? Why would you do it?"

4. How does a single-person god differ from the triune God in character and activity?

CHAPTER 2

GOD'S GLORY
The Radiance of the World

O God, I have tasted Thy goodness, and it has both satisfied me and made me thirsty for more.

A. W. TOZER

Just as God is a fountain who overflows with super-abundant love, so also is He a beacon of light shining into a dark world. Yet God doesn't just beam His light across the surface of the planet. He doesn't just shine it into dark nations and cities and continents where the gospel is relatively unknown. No, dear friend, our God also shines His light into the darkest of dark corners: the human heart. He opens up that dismal dungeon with the rays of His radiance and the luminance of His love. And this interior work is not just for the new believer, but also for the longtime Christian who has already found God. Both of these experience a divine work on their hearts.

THE SPIRIT'S DIVINE WORK

Which person of the Trinity performs this ministry? It is the special role of God's Holy Spirit. The first and primary work of the Spirit is to change our hearts. Romans 5:5 tells us, "God's love has been poured into our hearts through the Holy Spirit who has been given to us." And the way He particularly does this is seen in John 15:26. "When the Helper comes," said Jesus, "the Spirit of truth . . . he will bear witness about me." That, my friend, is the essence of the work of the Holy Spirit. He changes not just the surface level of our behavior, but goes deep down in our hearts, transforming what we love, what we desire, what we want. And He does it by opening our eyes to see Jesus.

I begin this chapter with a focus on the Spirit because this is my deep and abiding hope for you: I want the Spirit to open your eyes to see Jesus. To see our triune God more clearly so that you don't just feel a superficial buzz of excitement, you don't just find some tidbit of information that can serve as a life hack, but that your very heart quakes and melts, and you find God to be more satisfying than anything else.

Can a mere book do such a thing? Can reading just a single chapter transform you today? No, the book itself cannot—but the Holy Spirit can use even a bit of writing like this. I long to see an eternal ripple flow out from this chapter. I long to see God's glory shine out across the world, but I know it's got to start with our hearts being changed. And so as you read, say in your thoughts—or maybe out loud—"Father, change my heart. Make Jesus more satisfying and more delightful to me than anything else. Open my eyes that I may see Your glory and be changed. In Jesus' sweet and strong name I ask for this great gift." And because you have asked, may He do so!

THE GLORY OF GOD . . . IS GOOD

In this chapter, I want the Spirit to open our eyes to the radiant glory of God. I wonder what you think of when I use that fancy word, *glory*. It's one of those theological terms that we bandy around so freely. When you think of the glory of God, do you think of power, immensity, holiness? Often we can be very confused as to what to the glory of God means. But in Exodus 33:18, we read a great surprise. Moses said to the Lord, "Please show me your glory." And how did God reply? Amazingly, the Lord said, "I will make all my *goodness* pass before you." Unlike other gods whose glory might be about absolute power, the glory of this God is pure, radiant goodness. And in other Scriptures we learn of His glorious traits such as love, kindness, compassion, graciousness, and mercy. God's glory is to be *good* to mankind.

THE STORY OF CREATION, THE STORY OF MISSION, IS A STORY OF GLORY.

One man who understood God's glory was Jonathan Edwards, the prolific New England pastor and theologian from the 1700s. (I should also mention that he served for a number of years at a mission to Native Americans in Massachusetts. So in addition to everything else, he was a missionary.) Listen to what he said about how God is experienced in the radiance of His holiness. You probably recall several places in the Old Testament when people said, "We've seen God. Now we will surely die." Why is that? Why would they die? Edwards has an explanation, and it's surprising. He says,

> God is arrayed with an infinite brightness, a brightness that doesn't create pain as the light of the sun pains the eyes to behold it, but rather fills with excess of joy and delight. Indeed, no man can see God and live, because the sight of such glory would overpower nature, . . . 'tis because the joy and pleasure in beholding would be too strong for a frail nature.[1]

Did you catch that? Why is it that, if you saw God, you would collapse? It's not what you might think. It's not because you'd be incinerated like the trash. Edwards says we'd fall apart because of an excess of joy and delight. We would be so happy that we'd burst. That is who our God is. If you think He's remotely boring—oh, my friend, stop right now and pray that your eyes might be opened. Learn that God is so delightful that if you were to see Him purely unveiled, you'd explode with happiness.

I want to look at that glory now. The story of creation, the story of mission, is a story of glory. And it is a splendor well worth beholding.

The Light of God's Glory

At the very beginning of creation, God speaks into the darkness. Genesis 1:2–3 says, "The earth was without form and void, and darkness was over the face of the deep. . . . And God said, 'Let there be light,' and there was light." Do you see what God does when He speaks? We usually think of speaking words as something only audible, but here, it is also visual. God sends out His Word who is the glory of God. As John 1:5 tells us, this Word is a light that shines into the darkness and overcomes it. This Word is "the true light, which gives light to everyone" as it comes into the world (John 1:9). Can you imagine it? That's the very beginning of the universe: light is spoken into the darkness, and the light begins to drive away the darkness. And then by the end of the world, in Revelation 21 and 22, we learn that those future people do not need the light of a lamp, or sun, or moon; for the glory of God will give light to the new city—the new heavens and the new earth—and there will be no night anymore. The glory of God will fill all things, drive away the darkness in our hearts and in the world. So God's grand biblical narrative is a story of glory. And that glory is pictured by light.

Now you could say, "Well, every god wants to see their glory win." So the question is, what exactly *is* this glory of this God? What does it consist of? And for the triune God, it's a surprising kind of glory. The word "glory" in Hebrew in the Old Testament has to do with heaviness, or weight. It's about substance. So for example, our friend Eli the priest who raised Samuel—who's an old man by this point—falls backward off his stool and breaks his neck. Why? Because he is, we read in 1 Samuel 4:18, *heavy*. That's the same word. *Glorious* means weighty and substantial. The heaviness, the gloriousness of God, is His substance, who He is.

So then we might wonder, is God's heaviness something intimidating, like a playground bully? Or is it dull and ponderous and slow, like a lumbering, dim-witted ox? Not at all. Let's try to understand what the glory of God is like according to Scripture. Because if you get this—and my own experience in getting this helped me so much—if you truly see the glory of God and you appreciate the weight of God, He becomes more satisfying to you than anything else. You fix your eyes on heaven. And I'd love for you to be able to discover with me that even heaven would not be heaven without Him. God is the anchor of heaven and earth.

Ezekiel 1 is a marvelous chapter in the Bible. In it, we read of the throne-chariot of God approaching Ezekiel in glory. The prophet sees it as he's standing by the Kebar River. And on the throne was, according to verses 26–28, "a figure like that of a man . . . and brilliant light surrounded him. Like the appearance of a rainbow in the clouds on a rainy day, so was the radiance around him. This was the appearance of the likeness of the glory of the LORD" (NIV). Do you see? The appearance of the glory of God looks like a man and like a bright light. Let's look at these two things.

First of all, the light. Now, again and again in Scripture, you see God's glory being compared to light. "Then the glory of the LORD rose from above the cherubim and moved to the threshold of the temple. The cloud filled the temple, and the court was full of the radiance of the glory of the LORD," says Ezekiel 10:4 (NIV). And we read in Ezekiel 43:2, "Behold, the glory of the God of Israel was coming from the east. And the sound of his coming was like the sound of many waters, and the earth shone with his glory." Or Isaiah 60:1 cries to us and says, "Arise, shine, for your light has come, and the glory of the LORD has risen upon you." Light is the theme in each of these Scriptures.

And that night outside Bethlehem, can you picture the shepherds in the darkness watching their flocks? What does the gospel tell us? "The glory of the Lord *shone* around them" (Luke 2:9). Or when Jesus' disciples at His transfiguration saw His glory, what did it look like? "His face *shone* like the sun" (Matt. 17:2). Pure, unspotted, radiant. And at the end of all things, as we have seen, the eternal city does not need the light of lamps, for the glory of God gives it light (Rev. 21:23; 22:5). So the glory of God is like radiant light, shining out, enlightening our souls, giving life to our bodies, because the glory of the biblical God is radiant and outgoing; that is His nature. Not grasping or taking, but outgoing, generous, and loving. He's not about taking from us. This light radiates benevolent love. As the Puritan John Owen said, "Love is the light and glory which are about the throne on which God sits."[2] So the glory of God is like a shining light.

But in Ezekiel 1, we also saw that the appearance of God's glory looks like a man. And in fact, Ezekiel 3:23 even says, "The glory of the LORD *stood* there." The glory is pictured as a standing man, a person with feet. The radiance of God is seen in the form of a Man. Or as Hebrews 1:3 puts it, "The Son is the radiance of God's glory" (NIV). The Son, the Light of the World, is the splendor of the Father. He is the out-shining of the Father's bright glory.

Jesus, the Heart of God's Glory

Some people today can feel positive toward Jesus, who was the friend of sinners, but they imagine the "Old Testament God" as someone else, someone much more scary and nefarious. No, my friend. If you ever think that behind Jesus is some other being who is less lovely, who is lacking compassion and grace—well, you've not grasped that Jesus is the radiance of God's glory. There is no God in heaven who is unlike Jesus. Jesus *is* the glory of God, the very substance of His being. He is the radiance of His Father who shows us exactly what His Father is like. Jesus reminds Philip, "Whoever has seen me has seen the Father" (John 14:9). As you see Jesus' compassion as He groans over the sorry state of the leper or the widowed mother, as you see Him befriending and forgiving tax collectors and sinners: that is the glory of God. That is the very heart of God displayed. There is no other God secretly in heaven who is unloving and ungracious.

It is when Jesus comes down to us from heaven that we really see what God's glory is like. His glory surprises us because we expect it to be transcendently overpowering, but instead, it is so humble. Think about how Jesus shows His glory: in compassion, in stepping down from a place of prominence and power. That's how the glory of God comes to us, when the Prince of

> **THAT'S HOW THE GLORY OF GOD COMES TO US, WHEN THE PRINCE OF HEAVEN STEPS DOWN TO BE WITH EVEN US IN OUR DIRT AND SHAME.**

heaven steps down to be with even us in our dirt and shame. Of course, it's not just about dusty feet and dreary endurance. Jesus celebrates with His people and shares good things with them. He shows His glory as He changes water into wine. He shows His glory as He raises Lazarus from the dead. And the Spirit glorifies Him by taking what belongs to Jesus and sharing it with His followers (John 16:14). Do you see? His glory is all about sharing what is His—even sharing His sonship, His relationship with His Father. And all that leads up to the crux of history, the greatest moment in the whole timeline of the universe: the hour of Christ's glorification.

Would you come with me to John 12? I'd encourage you to put the book down for a moment, find a Bible, and gaze upon this passage. I love John 12, particularly from verse 21, and I'll tell you why. In the church where I used to minister in central London there was a big pulpit right at the center, with seating and balconies all around. And as you were about to preach, you would climb up to the pulpit, and right there, where no one but the preacher could see it—right in front of your eyes as you ascended to open the Word of God—you would see the words of John 12:21. It was what a band of Gentile foreigners said to Philip: "Sir, we wish to see Jesus." And as I would climb up into the pulpit, those are the words I would see addressing me as well: "Michael, we wish to see Jesus." That's what I am to do as a preacher. Not show you *me*. Do not look at *me*. Look to *Jesus*. And that's what we're to do as believers. People don't want to see you, they want to see Jesus. "Sir, we wish to see Jesus." What a motto for life!

But read on in John 12. In the verses afterward, Jesus says, "The hour has come for the Son of Man to be glorified" (v. 23). What does he mean? "Truly, truly, I say to you, unless a grain of wheat falls into the earth and dies, it remains alone; but if it dies, it bears much fruit" (v. 24). And in case there's any confusion, John says quite plainly in verse 33: "He said this to show by what kind of death he was going to die." You see, Jesus, the Son of Man, is the glory of His Father, and the cross—this terrible place of agony and shame!—is the hour of His glorification. My friend, this is the deepest revelation into the heart of God. Glory is found at the cross, when God was naked and bloody and mocked and shrieking in torment. No other god would want such glory. But here, revealed in Jesus Christ, is a God whose glory is found in giving out, in laying down His life to bear fruit. The triune God isn't about taking—He's about giving. And this changes entirely what mission is about and how we understand who it's for.

The Outgoing Glory of God

Mission is the outworking of God's very nature. Before we ever did anything for Him, this God comes and gives His life away for us. So mission does not start with something we do, but with something done for us. Mission, for us, is about entering into the gift of life before we have anything to give away. And that is why John's gospel really reaches its climax in chapter 20. If you still have your Bible open—I hope you took my advice before and have a copy before your eyes—if you have it, look at chapter 20. What do we find there? One of perhaps the two greatest mission passages in all of Scripture, where the Light of the World calls His people to be a light to the darkness. Jesus is the glory of God, shining out from His Father, and He calls His people to be lights to the world.

The setting in John 20 is this. It is the evening of that first day of the resurrection. And in verse 21, Jesus says to the gathered disciples, "Peace be with you." Now pause on that for a moment. Do you remember the last time He saw them? What have they done since He last saw them? Run scared and scatter. The last thing Jesus said to them is that He would pray for them. He knew they would

> **MISSION HAS ALREADY STARTED BECAUSE OF WHO HE IS. AND FOR US, ALL WE HAVE TO DO IS JOIN IN. MISSION STARTED NOT IN SOME TASK LIST YOU HAVE TO PERFORM, BUT IN GOD'S LOVE TOWARD YOU.**

all betray Him. And He even said, all the while knowing they would betray Him, that He promises to pray for them. This is how kind our Savior is! He knows full well you're going to betray Him—maybe not long after you set down this book. He knows you're going to be unfaithful. Even so, He remains faithful.

And once they've betrayed Him, denied Him, abandoned Him, the Lord of the universe says to these guilty disciples who have now fixed their eyes on His resurrected body—the very first thing He says is what? "Oh c'mon, you didn't do very well, did you? What a bunch of losers you turned out to be." No, of course not. The first thing Jesus says to them is, "Brothers, no condemnation. Peace be with you." Imagine hearing that when you've outright betrayed Him! Your backstabbing was right there with what the Roman soldiers did with their thorns and their nails. But Jesus can say, "Peace be with you," because He's dealt with all their sin on the cross—it's over and done. As the old German word says: *Kaputt!* All their sins have been covered in His blood, and so He says to them, "'Peace be with you. As the Father has sent me, even so I am sending you.' And when he had said this, he breathed on them and said to them, 'Receive the Holy Spirit'" (20:21–22). Now the disciples will have the power they need as they are sent on mission.

Is that surprising? Is Jesus switching gears here, doing something brand new in the history of God's relations with humankind? No, because Jesus never does that. He only does what the Father does, and whatever that is, He offers it to us. He is a mediator who bestows on human beings what God has bestowed on Him. That's exactly what John 15:9 tells us: "As the Father has loved me, so have I loved you." Do you remember what we discovered in chapter 1 of this book? We learned that the main thing the Father does is love the Son, breathing out the Spirit of His love upon Him. But the Father also sends the Son into the world. And as the saying goes: like Father, like Son. Just as the Son is sent by the Father, so then, inevitably, the Son sends out His followers. Jesus sends forth His disciples as one who was sent Himself. And that, my friend, changes what mission is all about.

WHO CAN JOIN HIS MISSION?

I want you to get this, particularly you readers who are feeling inadequate for the task of mission. Perhaps that word seems like something for the high-achieving believers who can bear extra burdens in the spiritual life, but it's not for an average Christian like you. But let's think about this. It's not as though God sits in heaven and just gives out an order: "Right, you folks there, you go out and do the hard work of mission. Somebody's got to do it. Might as well be you." I think we can often feel that that's how it is. Mission is for the self-starters and the extroverts, right? It's for those who can stand up and speak in public, and they've got all the words that seem to just come to them when they're speaking with people. It's for the professionals, because that's what they're supposed to be doing, isn't it? And you think, "I'm not like that. You know, I stumble over my words. I don't know what to say to people. I'm shy in front of people—I'm not an evangelist, and neither am I someone who can speak easily about God."

Oh, but it's so different with this God. Mission has already started because of who He is. And for us, all we have to do is join in. Mission started not in some task list you have to perform, but in God's love toward you. As His glory—His light—has begun to scatter your darkness first and foremost. God in His wholeness has already begun to mend your brokenness.

But maybe you're not shy. Could it be you really are high-powered? Then this may be the most important thing I'm going to tell you in this whole book. If you are that person who's confident in yourself, and you think, "Yeah, I'm going to go out and change the world. I can do this! I'll go to the ends of the earth and make it happen. And also, not to be prideful"—you say this part to yourself—"but Jesus should be honored to have someone like me on His team!" Oh, dear friend, I think you're going to have some hard times coming. I think you will be broken. You'll go out, all right, but you're going to burn out. Because mission is not about self-starters going out in their own energy. In fact, quite the opposite. You have to be broken and realize you are completely inadequate.

But take heart! Here's the encouragement for those who feel inadequate: God usually uses us most powerfully at the point of our brokenness. You might think, "I've got certain gifts, and I can offer those to God. But I've also got this very bruised area of my life. Or this very messed-up area of my life. And I know the Lord will use my good traits, but He's not going to use that scuffed-up part of me, or that secret garbage of mine." My friend, it might well be the other way around. Most often the Lord uses us at the very greatest point of our brokenness and our weakness. He's not after self-starters who go out in their own energy, strong and confident in themselves. That's not the gospel. Rather, brokenness is the main qualification for effective service.

If you feel your brokenness, your failure as a Christian, you are the person who qualifies for Jesus' help. Because you're broken, because you're a failure—that doesn't mean you don't qualify for Jesus; that *is* your qualification. So come to Him in your brokenness. Maybe even come right now. (Do you need to get on your knees? If so, don't hesitate.) Come to God in your brokenness and have His glory, His love, His mercy mend you.

Only then will He begin to use even that brokenness you feel so acutely. In fact, it may be the very thing that allows you to minister to others who are broken.

What does the world really need? Another perfect person like every influencer on social media, every actor in Hollywood, every sports star, every one of the glitterati with their looks and their wealth and their expensive toys? Even another celebrity Christian? No, the world needs to hear that God's glory isn't some triumphalistic power trip for the rich, slick, and successful. Here is a God who bows low, who deals kindly with our messes and heals our failures. And you—even you!—can go out and offer that to the world.

Friend, brokenness is a qualification for Christian service. It can make you far more happy in mission; far more compassionate; far more Christlike; far more fruitful. Such is the strange, upside-down world of the gospel. It means that because of the nature of this God in mission, when we go out and share His love, we're joining in and reflecting something profound about who God is. When we join Him in going out compassionately sharing His love for the world, declaring Him and His redemption, we're sharing His outgoing, generous life.

HE DWELLS OUTSIDE THE CITY

I have been sharing so many Scriptures with you that are on my heart. May I take you to another? It is one that reminds us of something important about Jesus. In Hebrews 13:12, we read, "Jesus also suffered outside the gate in order to sanctify the people through his own blood." Jesus endured a bloody execution outside the gates of Jerusalem, on the hill known as the Place of the Skull where the Romans crucified people beside the main road. What is important about this? It shows us that Jesus was willing to go—of His own free will, though He was taken by the soldiers—beyond the comfortable place, the place of homes and safety and civic life. He went beyond where the people of God are to a place of exclusion and shame. And He did this to make God's people holy through His own blood.

What is our response? Let us also go to Him outside the gate. Where is He to be found? Not on the inside where things are tame and quiet. No, the Lord Jesus is "out there." You only find Him by going out, not when you're comfortable and sitting back. Jesus is the one who went out first, in love for you. And the Christian life consists of being where He is. Going outside where it's risky. Going to the place of rejection, where there are crosses and trash heaps and bandits and tombs. All of that is what was outside ancient Roman cities. And yet Jesus went there willingly. So should we.

I would like to take you to another Scripture: Matthew 9:36–38, which is a famous mission passage. I want you to notice how weird this is. It's familiar to us, but also weird when you think about it. "When [Jesus] saw the crowds, he had compassion for them, because they were harassed and helpless, like sheep without a shepherd. Then he said to his disciples, 'The harvest is plentiful, but the laborers are few; therefore"—here's the strange part—"pray earnestly to the Lord of the harvest to send out laborers into his harvest.'" Why is that weird? Because it's Jesus

Christ, the Son of God—so why does He have to get help from others through praying? Wouldn't just one simple prayer of the Lord be far more effective than all their prayers combined? So who cares if they pray? Why doesn't He just pray for this Himself?

The answer, of course, is that He wants them to join Him. He wants them to be coworkers, fellow participants in the divine life, sharing His loving, compassionate, outgoing life. He wants us to join with Him in leaving the city and going out to the fields of harvest. And that is what makes the difference between reluctant or self-motivated mission that will fail, and joy-filled, grateful, joining-in mission. Cooperation with God's great purposes—not duty—is what makes the difference.

OVERFLOW WITH THE ENJOYMENT OF HIM

The English Puritan Richard Sibbes, who lived four hundred years ago, said that Christians singing God's praises are like the birds piping out their morning anthems. He wrote:

> As the shining of the sun enlargeth the spirit of the poor creatures, the birds, in the spring time, to sing, so pro-portionably, the apprehension of the sweet love of God in Christ enlargeth the spirit of a man, and makes him full of joy and thanksgiving. He breaks forth into joy, so that his whole life is matter of joy and thanksgiving.[3]

What did he mean? You know how it is at nighttime when things are dark and cold: the birds are quiet; they hunker down

OUT OF THE OVERFLOW OF OUR HEARTS, WE WILL SING BEFORE ALL THE WORLD OF A GLORIOUS REDEEMER.

in their nests. Just so with Christians. When they are dark and cold, they are quiet. But then the sun rises, and the light shines on those little birds and warms them. Their feathers fluff up, and they flap their wings. And then they begin to sing their hearts out in the dawn chorus. And just so, said Sibbes, the light of God's love shines on Christians. Let them bask in the sunshine of God's love and they will sing their hearts out for Jesus.

Mission is the overflow of love from the enjoyment of divine fellowship. As we partake in the Father's pleasure in His Son, and the Son's pleasure in His Father, and the Spirit's enlivening of their mutual love, it causes us to share their love for the world. Thus we become like what we worship. It is then, friend, you will want to sing of Him: when you are basking in the sunshine of God's love. Because, as Jesus said, the "mouth speaks from the overflow of the heart" (Luke 6:45 HCSB).

If you don't love God and you try to go on mission, people will hear of a God that you don't love, so why are they going to want that? But the work of the Spirit is to open our eyes to see Jesus in all His glory, to see God as He truly is. Touched by divine glory and the sunshine of God's love, out of the overflow of our hearts, we will sing before all the world of a glorious Redeemer. And in that moment when you do that, when you sing heartily of Jesus' great love for people who are failures—when you're able to know, "Yes, I'm a failure, and Jesus has loved me anyway"—then you begin to sing for real. That song has true power! You become like God, full of joy, full of life, full of fruit.

What are you living for? What do you love? Can it give you real joy? My friend, I'm going to plead with you now, don't settle for idols when you can have the real thing. Stop living for anything less than the glory and graciousness of the triune God. Live and die for the glory of Jesus. Don't settle for a good career. It won't satisfy. Don't settle for comfort. It's boring. Don't settle for trying to be popular. The feeling is empty after a while. These things, if you buy into their allure now, will bite you and hurt you later—they are piffling, passing things that don't deserve your all-out commitment. Don't settle for them. Nothing is more satisfying, nothing is more delightful than the glory of God. Don't rob yourself by chasing something lesser. Instead, this day, choose to plant your flag and say, "I will live and I will die for nothing less than the glory of Jesus Christ."

On Reflection

1. The Spirit opens our eyes to the "radiant glory of God." What do we mean by the "glory of God"? What descriptive words can you find for God's glory from this chapter? How does God's glory fill you "with an excess of joy and delight," as Jonathan Edwards puts it?

2. How do Jesus' words in John 20:21—"Peace be with you"—reflect His kindness? And how does the next part of the verse when Jesus sends out His followers naturally flow from His kindness?

3. "If you don't love God and you try to go on mission, people will hear of a God that you don't love, so why are they going to want that?" is the author's reasonable question. Describe how your love of God and your going on mission are intertwined.

CHAPTER 3

GOD'S ABUNDANCE
The Barren Land of No Trinity

It makes sense that there is no sense without God.

EDITH SCHAEFFER

So far in this book, we have seen that the Trinity is the engine, the fuel of mission. It is because God is Trinity that God is love, which is the reason why we have any good news to proclaim. And it is because God is Trinity that God is outgoing, which prompts us to go out too—not as an onerous duty placed on our shoulders, but as our heart's natural response to God's first coming to us.

Now what I want to do in this chapter is think about the opposite: What are you left with if you don't have Trinity? What do people who don't believe in a triune God have as a source of comfort or worship or reason for living? Vladimir Lossky, an

Eastern Orthodox theologian (1903–1958), once observed:

> If we reject the Trinity as the sole ground of all reality and all thought, we are committed to a road that leads nowhere; we end in an aporia [a despair], in folly, in the disintegration of our being, in spiritual death. Between the Trinity and hell there lies no other choice.[1]

He was absolutely right, and we're going to see why. We will see that such a place—the Land of No Trinity—is dry and dark. There is no light. There is no abundant water that gives productivity. No living things can come forth in such a barren wasteland. Nothing overflows. There is only the sterile, searing wind that sucks away the moisture of life and causes things to shrivel up and die. There is only lifeless sand—the hot desert without any refreshing sea breeze. The Land of No Trinity is a desolate and dreadful place. I mean it. This is no exaggeration. Without the Trinity, life just isn't worth living.

Why not?

TWO GRIM OPTIONS

Let us imagine that in the beginning, before all things, there is no Trinity. What are you left with? There are basically two options. Either before all things there is some other god, but he (or it) isn't Trinity. And the second option is, there is no deity whatsoever, and you are left with nothing before all things. Everything came from nothing, like a Big Bang whose cause is inscrutable and whose workings are purely mechanical. That's it. Either there is a god but he's not Trinity, or everything just came randomly out of nothing.

Now, there are shades and complexities here in both of these options. For example, there are polytheistic systems, but even polytheistic systems follow the non-triune god route. Or there are the "out of nothing" hypotheses that propose some kind of causative impulse for our universe within an infinite multiverse. So our universe has a reason for existing according to some principle that remains outside the known laws of physics. But however you slice and dice it, basically everyone who is not Trinitarian will live under one of these two systems as stated above—either there is a god but he's not triune, or there is no god at all. And I want to look with you for a moment at what that looks like, to live under a non-Trinitarian system. So venture with me—if you dare—into the Land of No Trinity.

The Solitary God

So first of all, let's look at the scenario that there is a god, but he's not triune. What's it like to live in that world? The most famous example, of course, is Islam. And I'm going to do something that may not happen very often in a Christian book: I'm going to quote from the Qur'an. It is not that I validate those scriptures as true, even historically, much less theologically. Yet I'd like you to see exactly how Allah distinguishes himself from the God who is revealed in Jesus.

Many times, people like to say, "The God of the Bible, the God of the Qur'an—surely you're talking about the same being, right?" People hear that both monotheistic religions believe in a single, divine being who is the sovereign creator, and they assume that the Muslim and the Christian are both pointing to the same deity, just from different angles. But is that true? Well, don't take my word for it. Let's listen to exactly what the Qur'an says and let Islam speak for itself. Let the sacred scriptures of this religion define the being that it offers for worship. Let the religion define for itself what their deity is and what it isn't.

I apologize for what I'm going to type here. It is offensive to Christians because it is false and blasphemous. First example:

"Say not 'Trinity.' Desist, it will be better for you: for God is one God"—and here's the bit that's so offensive—"Glory be to Him: (far exalted is He) above having a son."[2]

Here is the second verse:

> Say: "He, Allah, is One.
> Allah is He on Whom all depend.
> *He begets not, nor is He begotten.*
> And none is like Him."[3]

Look at what the Qur'an goes out of its way to say. Allah is not a father ("He begets not"). And he's not a son ("nor is He begotten"). Allah is making as clear as he can that he is not the God of the Bible, that he is not three. He is not Father, Son, and Spirit. Allah is crystal clear: he wishes it to be known he is a different god.

But here is what I want to press into. What is Allah most essentially like? What can be known about his character? Before he created anything, what had he been up to? We raised this topic in a general way in chapter 1, but let's focus here on a specific religion, a specific deity. Unlike Father, Son, and Spirit, Allah has been solitary for all eternity. Thus he has had no one and nothing to love. For eternity! Love is not his heartbeat, for love requires an other to be the beloved.

Interestingly, the prophet Muhammad said that Allah has ninety-nine names, each of which are to represent an attribute of his. And one of those names could be translated "the loving." But you might think, "How could he be loving? For eternity, he's been by himself, right? So what does he have to love?" And Islamic theologians have tried to come up with answers to how that might work. There are two possible responses to this.

One is that Allah eternally loves his Qur'an, his word, which is an eternal word in heaven beside him. Well, okay, but that's not quite what we mean by love, is it? Loving a thing, that's more like a hobby. It's not a relationship. You can love cars. You can love your stamp collection. You can love fish and chips. But that is not the same as falling in love with your spouse, or holding your newborn in your arms. Those are intimate relationships with persons, not objects in which you have interest. And relationship is what we truly mean by the word "love."

The other more popular option among Islamic theologians is that Allah eternally looks forward to his creation and loves his creation in advance, before it even exists. But do you see the problem with that one? If that's why he's called "the loving" (because he loves his creation), then Allah *needs* his creation to be who he is: "the loving." He depends on his creation for one of his attributes. It's one of the small inconsistencies in Islam, where it's trying to articulate something it wants to say, but it actually needs to be Trinitarian to make sense as a coherent belief system. It is incoherent because a core tenet of this religion is that Allah does not need to rely on anything, and yet here, in this one way, he seems to be dependent on his creation to be what he is said to be.

Here is where I want to go with all this. The implications for Allah's character, since he isn't eternally and essentially loving, are problematic to say the least. Unlike the true God, Allah is called the source of evil as well as good. And though he can be described with positive titles such as "the compassionate" or "the merciful," some of his less attractive names are "the proud," "the destroyer," and "the best of deceivers." In fact, around twenty passages in the Qur'an tell us that Allah leads people astray, tricking them, perverting them. For example, he is the one who deceives Christians into falsely believing that Jesus died and rose again by substituting a lookalike man on the cross. Now if that is the one true God—the "best of deceivers"—what do you think faith in him looks like? You constantly remain unsure, indeed frightened of him.

HOW DIFFERENT EVERYTHING IS WITH THE TRIUNE GOD!

Let me tell you a brief story about Muhammad's successor, the very influential first caliph of Islam, Abu Bakr. Now Abu Bakr was personally promised a place in paradise by Muhammad himself. Sounds pretty cool, doesn't it? It's like the Muslim equivalent of Philippians 4:3, where Paul writes about Clement and those other fellow workers "whose names are in the book of life." I always think, "It must have been great to be Clement. No assurance of salvation problems for him. *Am I really saved?* he might have wondered. *Yep, it says right there in Paul's letter that my name is in the book of life. I'm good to go.* Must be nice! So Abu Bakr was given this sort of promise too, straight from Muhammad, that he would be in paradise. But even so, Abu Bakr remarked, "By Allah, I would not rest assured and feel safe from the deception of Allah even if I had one foot in paradise."[5] He clearly believed that Allah cannot be trusted.

Can I be very clear here? Please understand, I am not being rude or derogatory. I am simply quoting the words of the first caliph of Islam. This is not religious slander on my part. It's exactly what Islam wants you to believe about God. How different everything is with the triune God! With Allah, because he's not essentially loving, he doesn't care about telling the truth. He's willing to deceive if it furthers his own purposes, which is all that matters in the grand scheme of things. Therefore we can't trust him.

There are many other consequences as well, but you can see even this one point rolling out into Muslim society. The repercussions of having a god who is not eternally loving are terrifying. For one thing, a religion in which the god does not enjoy and take delight in having another beside him inevitably has a problem with women. With a god like this, society always leans toward being exclusively male without the counterbalance of communal femininity. The male side of things dominates, all alone. Thus the female is excluded, the female is veiled away, the female is inferior—not different but equal, but actually of less intrinsic value. It always happens. The gender dynamic will be power-based instead of love-based. Contrast this outcome with the God of the Bible, in whose image male and female were created (Gen. 1:27).

My friend, without the Trinity, religious people in the world are condemned to a bleak system of sterile power instead of abounding love. It isn't only reflected in Islam. All who would not be Trinitarian are forced to live in this dark and sterile land.

The Absence of the Divine

The single-person god has been portrayed throughout history in ways that are deeply unattractive to our culture. And this has been coming not only from other religions that are intentionally non-Trinitarian, but even from a kind of pseudo-Christianity that doesn't properly take the Trinity into account, so it presents God in terrible, unworthy ways. All this religious discontent is fueling in our culture the other option, which is now starting to dominate the modern mindset: the idea that we came out of nothing and there is no god.

ANTITHEISTS BELIEVE THAT IF GOD WERE TO EXIST, IT WOULD BE A VERY BAD THING FOR SOCIETY. AND THEIR REASONING IS FASCINATING.

Not long ago, we were dealing in our culture with the issue of atheism on the rise. Individual people or even whole regimes did not believe in any God. Today we're long past that. Now we are into *anti*theism. Let me explain what that means. Theism is the belief in a deity. The prefix *a*- means "without," while the prefix *anti*- means "against." So antitheism is different from atheism in that while atheism believes there isn't a god, antitheism hates the very idea that there *could* be a god. It isn't religiously neutral, but actively hostile against God and, by implication, against all who put forth the idea of a god. Why?

Antitheists believe that if God were to exist, it would be a very bad thing for society. And their reasoning is fascinating. So the late Christopher Hitchens, one of the more famous antitheists, had a go-to illustration he used several times, comparing his idea of God to "a kind of divine North Korea. . . . greedy for uncritical praise from dawn until dusk."[6] During an interview for a cable news program, he was discussing belief in God and said, "I think it would be rather awful if it was true. If there was a permanent, total, round-the-clock divine supervision and invigilation of everything you did, you would never have a waking or sleeping moment when you weren't being watched and controlled and supervised by some celestial entity from the moment of your conception to the moment of your death . . . it would be like living in North Korea."[7]

> **WHAT IF GOD IS FUNDAMENTALLY A KIND AND LOVING FATHER, AND HE ONLY EVER ACTS AS SUCH? WHO WOULDN'T WANT THAT? BUT MOST PEOPLE DON'T UNDERSTAND GOD THIS WAY.**

But do you see what his assumption is here? For Hitchens, God is scary and interfering, a being who's watching your every move, ready to jump on you and punish you for the smallest infringement of his arbitrary and domineering rules. The regime in North Korea really is like this, and in many other countries as well, where covert technology can surveil you; then the secret police swoop in and capture you for punishment. And in this way of thinking, God is even more powerful than wiretaps and internet monitoring. He sees everything, then gets you for it. Who in their right mind would ever want such a being to exist? Perhaps it's not that Hitchens has a problem with the notion that God could exist, but he has a definite problem with what he perceives to be His character. He hates the thought . . . and fair enough!

But think how the picture could change if God is not a heavenly snoop spying on you, not a dictator reading your emails and texts to find your treason. What if God is fundamentally a kind and loving Father, and He only ever acts as such? Then living under His roof is not like living in North Korea, but under loving and nurturing care. Who wouldn't want that? But most people don't understand God this way. They've gotten the idea that if He's all-powerful, that must be bad. And you know, what I find is that the atheists or antitheists are not alone in this in our culture. Today's popular turn to various alternative spiritualities, from New Age to neo-paganism to Wicca, or just plain old superstition—they all demonstrate this kind of fear. Routinely, people go to those faiths because they hate the idea of a personal God. In fact, they hate the idea of a personal God because they're thinking of that god as a single person without any affection for the one at His side. Such a god is all power, no love. And that really is unappealing! But it isn't who God is.

Quite often, I do university missions. One of my common experiences in doing university missions, in speaking and preaching the gospel on university campuses, is that the atheist society will turn up. It's no surprise to me. In fact, I encourage this to happen. And I can usually spot them because they look so gloomy. And they'll come to me and they want to debate. So they'll say, "We don't believe in God." What I like say is, "Okay. Could you tell me about the God you don't believe in? What's he like?" And what's so interesting is, time and again, when these guys describe the God they don't believe in, it sounds as though they're describing the devil. They describe a god who's all-power-but-no-love, capricious, self-focused, brutish, vindictive, bereft of tender concern. And if their notion of a god is not Father, Son, and Spirit, they're exactly right. So I like to say to them, "Well, I don't believe in that god either. I hate the idea of that god. Let me tell you about a very, very different God."

THE REVIVAL OF ANCIENT PAGANISM

Unfortunately, a cultural hatred for God because of ignorance about the Trinity is taking our society back to paganism once again. And it's a pagan culture that doesn't recognize truth. To see something of what it looks like, let us consider John 18:28–40. This is the famous scene when Jesus stands before Pilate, and it has a strikingly modern familiarity. This governor, Pontius Pilate, is a cultured, skeptical pagan. Now this man named Jesus comes face-to-face with His judge. And Pilate judges Him. Or perhaps more accurately—and this is where our culture is today—Pilate just ignores Him. So in John 18:33–38, Pilate asks Jesus if He's king of the Jews. And Jesus answers, "Do you say this of your own accord, or did others say it to you about me?" But this seems like theological hogwash to Pilate, who's more of a cut-to-the-chase kind of guy. He says, "Am *I* a Jew?" He's so not interested in theology. He wants to get down to the legal matters. "What have you done?" he asks. Jesus answers, "My kingdom is not of this world. If my kingdom were of this world, my servants would have been fighting, that I might not be delivered over to the Jews. But my kingdom is not from the world."

Now watch what Pilate does here. He tries to bring it back to what he thinks is the legal issue at hand. He sees the opening for possible treason, a crime against the Roman emperor. "So you are a king?" he asks. And Jesus replies, no doubt frustratingly for Pilate, "You say that I am a king. For this purpose I was born and for this purpose I have come into the world—to bear witness to the truth.

WHEN CONFRONTED WITH THE CONCEPT OF TRUTH, PEOPLE ASK, LIKE PILATE WITH A WAVE OF HIS HAND, "WHAT IS TRUTH?" AND THEY TURN AWAY. IT'S NOT THAT THEY'RE ACTUALLY ASKING THE QUESTION.

Everyone who is of the truth listens to my voice." Pilate says to Him, "What is truth?" You can almost see Pilate wave his hand and make a scoffing sound. And after he says this, he goes back outside to the Jewish mob. He's not listening to Jesus, not really trying to debate the meaning of life. He just asks the mocking question and walks off.

Two thousand years later, that spirit still marks our culture. Certainly it is true in Europe, where I live. European culture is skeptical and deeply averse to the truth, and because of this, it is syncretistically pagan. When confronted with the concept of truth—and don't you see this increasingly around us?—people ask, like Pilate with a wave of his hand, "What is truth?" and they turn away. It's not that they're actually asking the question. They're not really truth-seekers trying to find ultimate meaning or a moral code to live by. They see the whole thing as a futile task because truth is like an exploded dream of yesteryear to be sneered at. I am describing Europe, though some of this will be familiar in the United States as well. There are similarities between the two, but you need to know how much further gone things are in Europe. You need to know because if current trends continue, this is where America is headed as well.

Across the continent of Europe, in terms of church congregation sizes, American congregations would outstrip them twenty times over. So if you want to know what European churches are like, think of your own church, then take away nineteen of every twenty congregants. Whatever is left, that is what churches look like in Europe. Then take away their baseline knowledge of what the Christian faith is all about. Populate the churches with people who started out with a total ignorance of Christianity, people who had never heard the name "Jesus," who had never seen a church as a place of living worship, who knew nothing at all about the content of the Bible.

And you can also see some of the differences played out in politics. In America, for a presidential candidate to mention God, it would probably help their election chances. In the UK, it was over twenty years ago that British Prime Minister Tony Blair was asked about his faith. His press secretary jumped in, saying, "We don't do God." Mentioning "God" is not going to help you in Europe; instead, it's going to be a deterrent for your chances of getting elected. And the fact that Europe has returned to Pontius Pilate's skepticism toward truth means we have this ancient pagan's problems in modern times.

> SOCIETY HAS LOST THE TRUTH THAT COULD GIVE IT COHERENCE. AND PEOPLE, NO LONGER LIVING IN GOD'S ORDERED WORLD, ARE FEELING THEY ARE IN A CHAOTIC AND TERRIFYING UNIVERSE. ONLY WITH THE TRINITY DO WE HAVE A WONDERFUL, COHERENT MEANING TO REALITY.

I'm a Brit, so please allow me to give you a bit of advice from the other side of the pond. My friend, be aware: here is what's coming your way in America. People want this departure from God because it seems like freedom. It's a bit like a child who runs away from home. Such an escape feels liberating at first, but then night falls and things turn menacing. Then being safe at hearth and home doesn't seem so bad anymore. But unlike the child who returns home with a renewed gratitude for his parents and his warm bed, today's religious seekers aren't interested in a homecoming. They're plowing ahead without God, come hell or high water (and they might find both!). They value their freedom so much, they're willing to forgo the comforts that God offers so they can chart an independent course in life.

And it truly is sad. In the new paganism, there is no gracious caretaker to look after you. There is no sovereign God steering creation toward purposeful ends. There is no loving acceptance by a heavenly Father. There is no hope. You are unloved, unprotected, and alone. And with God removed and rejected, people are adrift on an endless sea of meaninglessness. Society has lost the truth that could give it coherence. And people, no longer living in God's ordered world, are feeling they are in a chaotic and terrifying universe, caught in the machinery of impersonal, pitiless forces. And so people are troubled, dissatisfied, and desperately distracting themselves.

THE GOOD NEWS: RESCUE FROM A DREADFUL LAND

Do you see how terrifyingly sad it is when you don't have the triune God? You are forced to live in the Land of No Trinity, a land where there is no hope. This is where the peoples of the world live when they don't have our God. They're either with a false god who can't be trusted, one you'd be terrified of, or else no god at all. Absurdity abounds. Everywhere you look, you find meaninglessness. Only with the Trinity do we have a wonderful, coherent meaning to reality. Only with the Trinity do we have a God who loves us before we are ever worth it. Only with the Trinity do we have a message that people would want to hear, something other than, "God's going to smite you unless you follow His arbitrary rules," or "Nothing matters. Your life has no ultimate purpose."

In light of all this, I hope you can see how the Trinity is not only the fountain of mission, not only the impetus for spreading of the gospel, but is a truth we must speak about in our day-to-day evangelism. As we talk with people who say that all the religions of the world are the same, we can say, "No, let me show you how different the triune God is to all other gods. His character is so distinct. Here's how." Talking with Muslims, you can say, "Why would I want to be a slave of Allah, which is the best you can be, when I can be a beloved child of God my Father?" When meeting Jehovah's Witnesses who have a "single-person Jehovah," it's no surprise that in their circles, of course, you need to earn your salvation. Works are essential because their Jehovah isn't inclined to be merciful, and you'll never be his child.

But the triune God is so different from all the false gods of the world. And the atheists and antitheists who hate the idea of God, are they beyond reach? Not at all. You just need to show them that their view of the Christian God is more like what we call Satan. Instead, we can tell them of a God beyond their wildest dreams, one who is lovely and not horrifying as they have always dreaded.

KNOWING THE GOD OF MISSION

We Christians have, in the Trinity, a God the world needs to hear about. But to speak of Him, we first need to press in and know Him ourselves. I think this is one of the battles of the Christian life. Don't you find that so easily your view of God starts becoming less than biblical? You think that God is less loving, less gracious than He actually is. And here's a litmus test for this tendency: Have you ever felt, "Surely God will love me *once I sort myself out*"? That's a non-Trinitarian understanding of God, a graceless god like those of the world religions.

In fact, I'm going to dare to say that this statement is a satanic inversion of the gospel. For with this God who eternally experiences love within His own triune community of Persons, this God *is* Love, so He loves us before we ever sort ourselves out. When we were in the deepest pit of mess, that's when He came. That's when the Lord Jesus Christ came to die for us. Don't ever think there's any part of Christianity where you have to impress Him to earn your way in. Before you were even born, He reached out and completely paid for all sin—the sin of His beloved people. Don't buy that reversal of the gospel, that God will love you only when you make yourself more attractive. Remember what we read from Martin Luther, that sinners are attractive *because* they are loved. You're loved first, and that's what makes you love Him in response.

> **WHEREVER IT IS YOU'RE GOING TO GO, WHETHER ACROSS THE OCEAN OR ACROSS THE STREET, TELL PEOPLE OF THIS GOD.**

This is why the message of such a gracious God is what we have to take out to the world, to the masses of people ignorant of who God really is. The inversion of the gospel is all they know, so it is all they can live with. And that is so sad. I'm not just talking about far corners of the world where Christianity seems to have barely made a dent. I'm also talking about places where the gospel once was known and now is largely forgotten. Europe, which once sent so many missionaries across the world, is now considered by many missiologists as one of the most challenging places on earth to reach with the gospel. The situation is desperate in my homeland. And I have to say, friend, if you're considering, "Perhaps I should give my life to go out and tell others," please consider Europe. But wherever it is you're going to go, whether across the ocean or across the street, tell people of this God. However you're going to do it, let who God is shape how you're going to live and how you're going to go on mission.

On Reflection

1. As an example of other religions' understandings of deity, how does Allah, the god of Islam, differ from the God of the Bible in his relationship with his creation?

2. What is an atheist? an antitheist? Describe the kind of god an atheist or antitheist tends to portray.

3. Describe the barren place the universe would be without a triune God. How does a misbelief in who God truly is lead to absurdity and meaninglessness? Put into words ways of describing how the triune God is different from all others as though you were explaining to a friend.

CHAPTER 4

GOD'S LIGHT
Shining in the Darkness

Men have a great deal of pleasure in human knowledge,
in studies of natural things; but this is nothing to that joy
which arises from this divine light shining into the soul.
This spiritual light is the dawning of the light of glory
in the heart.

JONATHAN EDWARDS

Mission: so often it's a guilt word, right? Something we ought to do but are poor at. So sometimes we try to jazz ourselves up or make grand resolutions. But most of the time, we just feel guilty, knowing we're not like Jim Elliot, the celebrated missionary who was martyred in Ecuador. We're not like Amy Carmichael, who sacrificially served as a missionary in India for fifty-five years. We're not even like that person in church or the coworker who speaks effortlessly of their faith, seamlessly bringing the Lord in to ordinary conversation. We're failures.

We're rubbish. And sometimes we even *like* adding to the guilt, going along to a good, convicting talk that urges us to go out on mission. And such talks can be great. But . . .

Guilt is a terrible motivation. Awful. Which is strange, because people use guilt to get us to do things all the time. People guilt us into giving to charity, and they guilt us into "doing" evangelism. But in the end, guilt is crippling. When guilt is our motivation, eventually the burden of guilt becomes too heavy to be borne, and we just run from the problem and hide our heads in the sand. When guilt is our motivation for mission, we'll give up on reaching out to the lost. It's just too much to bear; we can never do enough.

Now please don't mishear me: I'm absolutely not saying we shouldn't have compassion for the lost. Of course we should. God does. But I want to say that compassion is something very different from guilt. Guilt is a negative emotion. Having it is like carrying a corrosive acid inside you. If you have guilt, you're the one who needs help. You need Jesus to wash it all away. But compassion is the beautiful emotion of one who is full: full of love.

And what I want us to see now is how the children of God are given a whole new heartbeat. Instead of the old guilt-driven life, striving to achieve to fill the void and cure the hurt within, the children of God have a fullness to them. They have a love-driven and joy-fueled life.

SPIRIT-FUELED LIVING

Come with me to Romans 8, and let's start by seeing what the children of God are freed from. Verse 1: "There is therefore now no condemnation for those who are in Christ Jesus." Not *less* condemnation—*no* condemnation! And these ringing words are not a promise only for those who've sorted themselves out. This is for all Christians, all who have simply fled to be "in Christ Jesus."

Let's go on a bit to see what this means for our lives. Verse 12: "So then, brothers, we are debtors, not to the flesh, to live according to the flesh." Pause there: what is this "flesh" or "sinful nature"? It's easy to think the flesh or sinful nature is simply our tendency to do naughty things. So when Paul says we shouldn't live according to the flesh, we think he's saying "stop doing naughty things."

But no! The flesh means much more. In Galatians 4:21–31, Paul used the story of Abraham, Isaac, and Ishmael to understand "the flesh." Do you remember the story? In Genesis 12, the Lord promised Abraham (then called Abram) a son. But after ten years had gone by, Abraham started to wonder if Sarai, his wife, could ever conceive. So he decided to get God's blessing of a son *by his own effort*. He took Sarai's servant Hagar as a wife (Gen. 16). The result was a son, Ishmael.

But Ishmael was not the child of God's promise. The promised son, Isaac, was still to come. Ishmael was the child *of the flesh*. So when Paul writes of "the flesh," he means more than our natural tendency to do bad things. The "flesh" includes our instinctive attempts to bring about God's blessing all by ourselves, as Abraham brought about Ishmael. It means our natural attempts to buy God off and earn His favor. Our earn-it religiosity: *that's* the flesh.

And Paul says in verses 13–15 of Romans 8, "If you live according to the flesh you will die, but if by the Spirit you put to death the deeds of the body, you will live. For all who are led by the Spirit of God are sons of God. For you did not receive the spirit of slavery to fall back into fear, but you have received the Spirit of adoption."

Do you see the contrast? You can live by the flesh, which means living under a spirit of slavery, always propelled by an insatiable lack, by guilt, by greed, by the desire to justify yourself. Or you can live as a child of God, by the Spirit of adoption. We'll see the Spirit of adoption in a moment, but before then, I want us to get clear on this spirit of slavery, because it's everywhere. We fall back into this so easily, and it is a parasite on our joy, our peace, our love, and our life.

Exhibit A: The Venerable Dr. Johnson

So, spirit of slavery, Exhibit A: I give you Dr. Samuel Johnson, eighteenth-century literary giant, author of *A Dictionary of the English Language*, and poor enslaved man, chained to a spirit of slavery. To get inside his head and see this spirit of slavery at work, here are a few extracts from his *Prayers and Meditations*, his daily prayer journal.[1] See if any of this sounds familiar:

September 18, 1738

O Lord, enable me by Thy Grace to redeem the time which I have spent in sloth, vanity and wickedness; to make use of Thy gifts to the honour of Thy Name; to lead a new life in Thy faith, fear and love; and finally to obtain everlasting life.

January 1, 1757

Almighty God, . . . forgive me that I have misspent the time past; enable me, from this instant, to amend my life according to Thy holy word; grant me Thy Holy Spirit, that I may so pass through things temporal, as not finally to lose the things eternal.

Easter Eve, 1761

I have resolved (I hope not presumptuously) till I am afraid to resolve again. Yet, hoping in God, I steadfastly purpose to lead a new life. O God, enable me, for Jesus Christ's sake. My purpose is,

To avoid idleness.

To regulate my sleep as to length and choice of hours.

To set down every day what shall be done the day following.

To keep a journal.

To worship God more diligently.

To go to church every Sunday.

To study the Scriptures.

To read a certain portion every week.

April 20, 1764

I have made no reformation; I have lived totally useless, more sensual in thought, and more addicted to wine and meat. Grant me, O God, to amend my life.

September 18, 1764

I have now spent fifty-five years in resolving; having from the earliest time almost that I remember, been forming schemes of a better life. I have done nothing. . . . O God, grant me to resolve aright, and to keep my resolutions. . . . I resolve to rise early; not later than six if I can.

Easter Day, 1765

I purpose to rise at eight, because, though I shall not rise early, it will be much earlier than I now rise, for I often lie till two.

April 10, 1775

When I look back upon resolutions of improvement and amendment, which have year after year been made and broken . . . why do I yet try to resolve again? I try, because reformation is necessary, and despair is criminal. I try, in hope of the help of God.

Isn't it tragic? See his constant resolutions to do better in the hope that these will win him the right to everlasting life. He tries and fails, tries and fails, all the time becoming more and more weary with it all. That's the life of the flesh: Johnson indulges in the wine and meat he loves, and then guilt drives him to fleshly attempts to make himself a new man. It's all self-effort, with prayers then flung upward, asking for God to chip in and help his efforts. You can hear it: Johnson went through his life ground down with guilt. He just didn't realize his deepest problem: he wouldn't simply accept the free pardon and welcome of God. And so he tried to deal with his guilt by self-improvement.

Exhibit B: Caleb . . . and You

I wonder if you've been there. And I wonder if the directive to evangelize has been part of your guilt, one of those things you've resolved to improve but always experienced as a burden that makes you a failure.

Dear friend, that is not the life the children of God are called to! The child of God isn't to be driven by guilt. The child of God knows *no condemnation*. The child of God can look on Christ and say, "All my sin has been drowned in the blood of Christ. To rid me of my guilt is why He died." As Paul puts it in Romans 8:15, "You did not receive the [Samuel Johnson–like] spirit of slavery to fall back into fear, but you have received the Spirit of adoption as sons, by whom we cry, 'Abba! Father!'" Paul here is describing the new birth, how once we were born of the flesh, but now by the Spirit have been born again. This is what it means to be a Christian. Not to be born into a Christian culture, but born again into a living, personal trust in Christ. And for those who are born again, we have a new life with a whole new heartbeat. The Spirit brings us to share the Son's heartbeat.

THIS IS WHAT IT MEANS TO BE A CHRISTIAN. NOT TO BE BORN INTO A CHRISTIAN CULTURE, BUT BORN AGAIN INTO A LIVING, PERSONAL TRUST IN CHRIST.

Once I saw nothing attractive in God, but the Spirit has awakened me to share the tastes and the heartbeat of the Son. I have a new Spirit inside. I don't want to buy God off anymore.

I know I don't need do. Jesus has paid the price for all my sin. And so, like the Son, I now find I actually *love* the beautiful God who loved me first. I find myself crying, like Jesus, "Abba! Father!" (See Mark 14:36.) My love is not put on as an attempt to *earn* His love; it's a spontaneous *reaction* to His love for me.

The children of God have new hearts, and a new Spirit in them. And the Spirit we are given is the Spirit *of the Son* (Gal. 4:6). The One who blesses and empowers the Son comes to move on us in the same way. The One who makes the love of the Father known to the Son now makes that same love known to us, so that we too exclaim, "Abba!"

It all means that, just as the Son can act out of fullness, filled to overflowing with love, so we are liberated to live. Not trying to get, for we've been given everything. The children of God live from fullness: fullness of love, fullness of blessing, of life, of joy.

Let me illustrate what this looks like with one of my favorite Old Testament characters. He is one of the few people in the Old Testament who is repeatedly said to have followed the Lord fully or wholeheartedly (Deut. 1:36; Josh. 14). We first get to meet Caleb when he is sent by Moses to reconnoiter in Canaan as one of the twelve Israelite spies. There, he is described as being "from the tribe of Judah, Caleb the son of Jephunneh" (Num.13:6). It's not much, but it means we know two things about him: he is of the tribe of Judah, and his father is Jephunneh.

That may not seem very exciting, until you start seeing there's a puzzle here. For later he is called "Caleb the son of Jephunneh *the Kenizzite*" (Num. 32:12). His father is *not* from the tribe of Judah, but is a Kenizzite. And the Kenizzites were one of those scary tribes of *pagan* Canaanites (Gen. 15:19). So Caleb is an ethnic Gentile, not a native Jew. Almost certainly that explains his name, for Caleb means "dog" in Hebrew, and the Israelites commonly referred to foreigners as "Gentile dogs." Like Rahab, Ruth, and many others, a Gentile "dog" had joined Israel and been adopted into the royal tribe of Judah. Though born a pagan, he would receive an inheritance as a part of Judah (Josh. 15:13). Indeed, of all the wilderness generation, it was only Joshua and Caleb who survived to enter the land: an ethnic Jew and an ethnic Gentile walking together and equal into God's reward.

> **JOSHUA AND CALEB . . . AN ETHNIC JEW AND AN ETHNIC GENTILE WALKING TOGETHER AND EQUAL INTO GOD'S REWARD.**

And here's the point: Is it a coincidence that this Caleb was repeatedly spoken of as wholehearted for the Lord? Surely not. He had been *adopted*, welcomed and embraced, and found he *belonged* with the Lord and His people. He was far less likely to fall into Baal worship and remained a lionhearted soldier of the Lord into his late eighties.

Adoption is a powerful and heart-affecting thing. It was for Caleb as a son of Judah, and it is for us as children of God. We have been shown such kindness, and now we belong with our Father. Those who know themselves to be welcomed by the God who is Father, Son, and Spirit are wholehearted like no others.

So Much Does Our Triune God Have to Give

In this book, we have seen again and again that we are loved by a God who is a loving Father of a beloved Son in the life-giving love of the Holy Spirit. What the triune God offers us, then, is not just forgiveness, not just acceptance, not just a declaration of innocence. Any aggrieved party can offer forgiveness and still maintain distance from the restored person. A coworker can forgive your miscue at the office. A judge in a law court can offer exoneration from the bench. A counselor can accept your deepest sins and fears in a clinical setting. But what the biblical God offers us is the Father adopting us into the same relationship that He has with His own Son. Did you catch that? We are brought into the very life of the Son of God! No other god offers such a thing because they can't. Since they aren't triune, these other gods don't have it to give.

If you're considering your part in the divine mission, have a think about this: Why is it that the Son goes on mission? In fact, why is it that the Son does anything? We must remember that the Son of God does not act out of guilt or a need to curry favor with His Father or anyone else. He lives, He acts, He comes into the world, He dies—and all because so much love has been showered on Him by His Father that He overflows with it. He cannot help but love His Father back and long to do His will. Brimming over with love, He pours it out on the world. That's how it is for the Son of God.

And that's how it is for all the children of God. For the same is true of you who have been adopted as a son or daughter of the living God. Don't think that you need to go on mission to impress God, to impress your pastor, to impress the spiritual people in your church. Don't do it for that reason. There's no need to buy God off. You can't do it anyway. Even if you tried, it wouldn't work. No, the Son of God goes out from His Father because so much love has been showered on Him that He overflows with it, and He cannot help but love His Father back in this way.

Listen again to the Son's own words in which he gushes with the joy of the Beloved. When Jesus was full of joy in the Holy Spirit, He cried, "I praise you, Father, Lord of heaven and earth" (Luke 10:21 NIV). And here's the amazing thing: that exact same love has been poured out on us too. Romans 5:5 says, "God's love has been poured into our hearts through the Holy Spirit who has been given to us." Not trickled. Not dribbled. Poured out, abounding. It means that just as the Son acted out of love when He came to our world, you do the same wherever you are sent as well. If you're to go on mission, you go not trying to get anything from God. Rather, you're going on mission because you've already been given all there is to get. The children of God live from a fullness of life, a fullness of blessing. We can't help but overflow with it. Other people need it too.

But what if you don't always feel that sense of abundance? That's when you go back to the promises of God and remember: "Yes, I have peace with God. Yes, death has no sting. Yes, we are His, bought with a price." And as you fill yourself up with the promises of God, you are reminded of your adoption into His family. The warmth of divine acceptance comes over you. The Spirit fills you with confidence. And as you begin to find that cry welling up in your heart, "Abba, Father!"—a name of intimacy—you go out again, filled to the brim with His love. I would love to see a new generation rise up and want to go to the ends of the earth in mission. But only if that generation is motivated by a fullness of delight in God. And so I want to ask: What would it look like if, instead of reluctantly going on mission as a bit of drudgery, we lived the Spirit-fueled lives of the sons of God?

THE MANY "SONS" OF GOD

If we're going to talk about the "sons of God," let's start right at the beginning and acknowledge the elephant in the room. What about the daughters of God? Isn't using the phrase "sons of God" sexist and exclusionary? Maybe even misogynistic? No, there is a very specific reason for using the term "sons."

Romans 8:14 tells us, "For all who are led by the Spirit of God are sons of God." And the reason Paul says that, and he doesn't mention daughters (though of course they are included) is because the apostle wants us to be clear that the status we are given is the status of the Son Himself. So female readers will have to figure out how to understand themselves in relation to a male image—how to be "sons" even though they are daughters. But, you know, guys are part of the bride of Christ according to Scripture. They have to understand themselves in relation to a female image! And the women get the very status of the beloved Son Himself, just like the men, nothing less than what Christ Himself has. Jesus is the Son, and we are all sons of God. It's an amazing privilege. But what does that look like?

You remember that back in chapter 2, we were looking at God's glory, His radiant nature. We saw that God is like a shining sun going out. But what is the sun? A star, of course—the biggest and brightest of them all in our experience. And that's why I think the image that Scripture gives us for believers is the stars. There are many stars in the night sky, billions of them, trillions, an uncountable number. And they are all fueled by basically the same mechanism that our sun is. The daytime sun is the powerful, overwhelming, blazing version of starry light, and we Christians are little suns that emit the same sort of light and shine it upon the world. Taken all together, we give a lot of illumination!

THAT IS HOW IT IS WITH CHILDREN OF GOD: THEY SHINE WITH LOVE AND JOY BECAUSE THEY'RE FILLED WITH LOVE AND JOY.

Jonathan Edwards said this: "The stars were designed by the creator to be a type [or picture] of the saints, the spiritual seed of Abraham. And the seeming multitude of them, which is much greater than the real multitude of visible stars, was designed as a type of the multitude of the saints."[2] Does that strike you as weird? It almost sounds pagan, doesn't it? I mean, fixating on the heavenly bodies, or giving them names like Mars and Venus, or taking horoscopes from the constellations of the zodiac and all that. It seems un-Christian. But what I'm talking about isn't that sort of thing. And it isn't pagan at all. Let's have a look at what Scripture says about this. "The stars were designed by the Creator to be a picture of the saints," according to Edwards. Is that really biblical?

In Genesis 15:5, do you remember what God does? The Lord leads Abraham outside and has him look up at the stars, and He says, "Number the stars, if you are able to number them. . . . So shall your offspring be." The chosen people, the children of promise, the offspring of Abraham. They are as innumerable as the stars. And now let's think about Job 38. I want you to get this image because it helps you see how to go out happily on mission. In verses 4–7, the Lord asks Job, "Where were you when I laid the foundation of the earth? Tell me, if you have understanding. Who determined its measurements—surely you know! Or who stretched the line upon it? On what were its bases sunk, or who laid its cornerstone"—and then get this, as it continues—"when the *morning stars* sang together and all the *sons of God* shouted for joy?"

See that connection? Stars, sons of God. Some translations say "the angels of God." That's not wrong, but the Hebrew text literally says "the sons of God shouted for joy." Angels are sometimes spoken of as sons of God in Scripture. Not because they are adopted like believers, but because, like the stars, they are designed by the Creator to be a picture of what we who are the true sons of God are like: a people shining in holiness, delighting to gather around the Lord in heavenly worship. Can you picture it? As the Lord fills the universe with countless stars, so He will fill His creation with the sons of God. They will gather around Him and, like the true Light of the World, they will shine with sparkling radiance as well.

Reflecting His Splendor

What an expressive image—His many sons, His many daughters, all reflecting the same splendor as the Son of God. Now I'm going to give you another Scripture passage, and you will see why this is a favorite of mine. Just read it and try to imagine the final resurrection at the end of time. Daniel 12:1–3 says,

> At that time shall arise Michael, the great prince who has charge of your people. And there shall be a time of trouble, such as never has been since there was a nation till that time. But at that time your people shall be delivered, everyone whose name shall be found written in the book. And many of those who sleep in the dust of the earth shall awake, some to everlasting life, and some to shame and everlasting contempt. And those who are wise shall shine like the brightness of the sky above; and those who turn many to righteousness, like the stars forever and ever.

Look at what that last bit says. Just as Christ is the Light of the World like we saw in the book of Revelation, so the sons of God shine light into the darkness. And they turn many to righteousness, pointing them to the true Source of life and light.

Why do stars shine? Not because they're desperately trying to, as if there's some lack in them. They aren't like a flickering flashlight whose batteries are dying. Just the opposite: stars shine because they're so explosively full of light and energy. They can't help but shine because radiance is bursting from them. And that is how it is with children of God: they shine with love and joy because they're filled with love and joy. Because they know, "Here is a God who loved me first, who loved me even in my brokenness, and who couldn't love me more."

Here's the last passage from the Bible I will share. In Philippians 2:15–16, Paul prays for the Philippians, and it's the same thing that I pray for you. It is why I have written this book. It is what I want you to take away. I pray "that you may become blameless and pure, 'children of God without fault in a warped and crooked generation.' Then you will shine among them like stars in the sky as you hold firmly to the word of life" (NIV). My friend, may you hold firmly to the word of life. May the love of Christ Himself, who is the Incarnate Word, be the sustenance of your soul. Then, in the darkness of this love-hungry world, those who are full of God's love, full of light, are like beacons of hope. The world will not just see an empty, black void. No, they will gaze up and see sparkling stars in the night. The sons of God are meant to be like the stars, the hosts of heaven, shining in the darkness of sin and depravity. And they shine because they offer the love and light of God Himself.

Allow me to close, not with Scripture, but with a quotation from J. R. R. Tolkien's *The Return of the King*. Sam and Frodo are in Mordor, the land of shadow. Sam looks up, and Tolkien describes his reaction to what he observes:

> There, peeping among the cloud-wrack above a dark tor high up in the mountains, Sam saw a white star twinkle for a while. The beauty of it smote his heart, as he looked up out of the forsaken land, and hope returned to him. For

like a shaft, clear and cold, the thought pierced him that in the end the Shadow was only a small and passing thing: there was light and high beauty for ever beyond its reach.[3]

Did you catch it in these resounding words? The light and high beauty is forever beyond the reach of the shadow. That is precisely what Jonathan Edwards meant when he said, "The stars were designed by the Creator to be a picture of the saints." In the Land of No Trinity, which is arid and dark and desolate, those who know the triune God are reminders of His presence. Their sonship points to the true Son of God, the Beloved of the Father, who offers adoption into the family of God. This good news is like water to a parched throat, like light to those groping in darkness. Your mission is to bring the hope of the gospel to desperate people.

Dear friend, thank you for turning the pages of this book with me. Thank you for hearing my heart. How I want you to know the unconditional love that the Father has for you! Then you will have a light within you that is the hope and desire of every man and woman, to be so loved. And where others can only see empty darkness, if you have fed on the great love of God, you will shine like a star, leading many to righteousness. You will radiate His compassion to the world. You will blaze forever and ever. But you will have that light only insofar as you know God. You could never get it from yourself or generate it from within. Yet as you come to know the gracious, compassionate, triune God, you can shine as a light in the darkness of this world until the glorious day when the shadow finally passes.

On Reflection

1. Caleb is said to have followed the Lord wholeheartedly. Can you say the same about yourself? (This is not a yes/no question, but an opportunity to give the matter some intentional thought!)

2. How is the world illumined?

3. Throughout the book, the author has stressed that we go on mission not out of guilt or duty or a desire to impress anyone. "Rather, you're going on mission because you've already been given all there is to get. The children of God live from a fullness of life, a fullness of blessing. We can't help but overflow with it. Other people need it too." How has this been your experience in evangelizing?

4. What is next for you?

NOTES

INTRODUCTION
KNOWING THE TRIUNE GOD

Epigraph: Carolyn Weber, *Surprised by Oxford: A Memoir* (Nashville: Thomas Nelson, 2001), 81.

1. C. H. Spurgeon, "The Immutability of God," *The New Park Street Pulpit Sermons*, vol. 1 (London: Passmore & Alabaster, 1855), 1.

CHAPTER 1
GOD'S LOVE: THE FOUNTAIN OF ALL GOODNESS

Epigraph: Katherine Elizabeth Clark, *Where I End: A Story of Tragedy, Truth, and Rebellious Hope* (Chicago: Moody, 2018), 36.

1. *The Complete Works of Richard Sibbes*, ed. A. B. Grosart, 7 vols. (Edinburgh: James Nichol, 1862), 6.113.

2. C. S. Lewis, *The Screwtape Letters* (Glasgow: Collins, 1942), 45–46, original emphasis.

3. Martin Luther, *Luther's Works: Career of the Reformer I*, vol. 31, ed. Jaroslav Jan Pelikan, Hilton C. Oswald, and Helmut T. Lehmann (Philadelphia: Fortress Press, 1999), 57.

CHAPTER 2
GOD'S GLORY: THE RADIANCE OF THE WORLD

Epigraph: A. W. Tozer, *A. W. Tozer: Three Spiritual Classics in One Volume* (Chicago: Moody, 2018), 228.

1. Jonathan Edwards, "That God is the Father of Lights," *The Blessing of God: Previously Unpublished Sermons of Jonathan Edwards*, ed. Michael McMullen (Nashville: Broadman & Holman, 2003), 346.

2. *The Works of John Owen*, ed. William H. Goold, 24 vols. (1850–55; republished, Edinburgh: Banner of Truth, 1965–91), 23.99.

3. *The Complete Works of Richard Sibbes*, ed. A. B. Grosart, 7 vols. (Edinburgh: James Nichol, 1862), 6.388.

CHAPTER 3
GOD'S ABUNDANCE: THE BARREN LAND OF NO TRINITY

Epigraph: This quote has been widely circulated and is attributed to Edith Schaeffer, who was an author and cofounder of L'Abri.

1. Vladimir Lossky, *The Mystical Theology of the Eastern Church* (Cambridge: James Clarke & Co., 1957), 66.

2. Surah 4:171. A surah is a chapter in the Qur'an, which contains 114 chapters.

3. Surah 112:1–4, my emphasis.

4. Surah 4:157.

5. Khalid Muhammad Khalid, *Successors of the Messenger: Allah's Blessing and Peace Be Upon Him*, translated by Muhammad Mahdi al-Sharif (Dar Al-Kotob Al-Ilmiyah: Beirut, 2005), bk 1, 99.

6. "Christopher Hitchens: 'A celestial dictatorship, a kind of divine North Korea', Munk Debate - 2010," November 26, 2010, https://speakola.com /ideas/christopher-hitchens-munk-debate-2010.

7. Christopher Hitchens, interview on *Hannity & Colmes*, Fox News, May 16, 2007.

CHAPTER 4
GOD'S LIGHT: SHINING IN THE DARKNESS

Epigraph: Stephen R. Yarbrough and John C. Adams, *Delightful Conviction: Jonathan Edwards and the Rhetoric of Conversion* (Westport, CT: Greenwood Press, 1993), 122. The quote is from Edwards's sermon "A Divine and Supernatural Light," preached in 1734.

1. Samuel Johnson, *Prayers and Meditations* (London: T. Cadell, 1785).

2. *The Works of Jonathan Edwards* (New Haven and London: Yale University Press, 2006), 157.

3. J. R. R. Tolkien, *The Lord of the Rings: The Return of the King* (London: George Allen & Unwin, 1966), 199.

CAN A CHRISTIAN EVER FINISH CONTEMPLATING THE TRINITY?

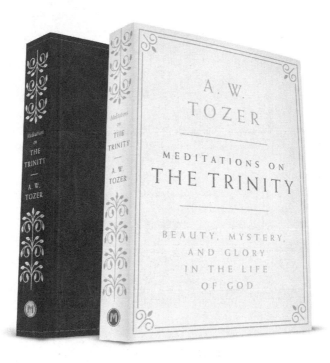

MOODY Publishers®

From the Word to Life®

Meditations on the Trinity is a compilation of excerpts from A. W. Tozer, arranged for daily reading. It consists of four parts: one part on each respective person of the Trinity, and one on God three-in-one. Together it offers a more accurate view of who God is, aiding readers in truer worship.

978-1-60066-803-6 | also available as an eBook

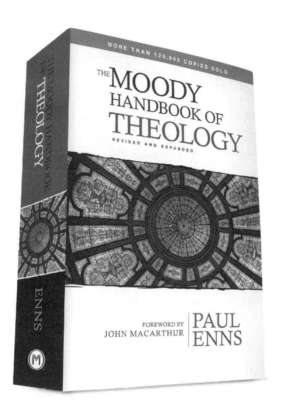